The NetRexx Language

M. F. Cowlishaw

To join a Prentice Hall PTR internet mailing list, point to http://www.prenhall.com/register

Prentice Hall PTR
Upper Saddle River, New Jersey 07458
http://www.prenhall.com

Library of Congress Cataloging in Publication Data

Cowlishaw, M.F.
The NetRexx language / M.F. Cowlishaw
p. cm.
Includes index.
ISBN 0-13-806332-X
1. NetRexx (Computer program language) I. Title.
QA76.73.N47C68 1997
005.13'3--dc21 96-45703
CIP

Editorial/production supervision: *Nicholas Radhuber*
Manufacturing manager: *Alexis Heydt*
Acquisitions editor: *Paul Becker*
Marketing manager: *Dan Rush*
Cover design director: *Jerry Votta*
Editorial Assistant: *Maureen Diana*

Published by Prentice Hall PTR
Prentice-Hall, Inc.
A Simon & Schuster Company
Upper Saddle River, New Jersey 07458

The Publisher offers discounts on this book when ordered in bulk quantities.
For more information, contact:

Corporate Sales Department
Prentice Hall PTR
1 Lake St.
Upper Saddle River, NJ 07458
Phone: 800-382-3419 Fax: 201-236-7141
E-mail: dan_rush@prenhall.com

Printed in the United States of America
10 9 8 7 6 5 4 3 2

ISBN 0-13-806332-X

Prentice-Hall International (UK) Limited, *London*
Prentice-Hall of Australia Pty. Limited, *Sydney*
Prentice-Hall Canada Inc., *Toronto*
Prentice-Hall Hispanoamericana, S.A., *Mexico*
Prentice-Hall of India Private Limited, *New Delhi*
Prentice-Hall of Japan, Inc., *Tokyo*
Simon & Schuster Asia Pte. Ltd., *Singapore*
Editora Prentice-Hall do Brasil, Ltda., *Rio de Janeiro*

For programmers everywhere

Contents

Preface

NetRexx is a new general-purpose programming language inspired by two very different programming languages, Rexx and Java™. It is designed for people, not computers. In this respect it follows Rexx closely, with many of the concepts and most of the syntax taken directly from Rexx or its follow-on, Object Rexx. From Java it derives static typing, binary arithmetic, the object model, and exception handling.

The first implementation of NetRexx produces classes for the Java Virtual Machine, and in so doing demonstrates the value of that concrete interface between language and machine: NetRexx classes and Java classes are entirely equivalent – NetRexx can use any Java class (and vice versa) and inherits the portability and robustness of the Java environment.

When I started designing NetRexx, it was an experiment: there was no guarantee that an 'Object Rexx for the Java environment' was viable. Critical areas of the design – notably the syntax for referring to types, and automatic conversions – took many iterations to get right, followed later by extensive tuning in response to feedback from the early users of the language. The result is a single language that not only provides the scripting capabilities and decimal arithmetic of Rexx, but also seamlessly extends to large application development with fast binary arithmetic.

More than a decade ago, I wrote that I hoped that future programming languages would improve on Rexx, and that Rexx was just a start in the direction of languages designed for people rather than computers. Although disappointingly little research has been carried out in this area in the interim, it was encouraging to discover that the philosophy behind the Rexx design can be applied so completely to a very different class of language, one both object-oriented and statically typed.

I believe that NetRexx is indeed an improvement on Rexx. Although Rexx has been widely used for 'mission critical', and sometimes quite enormous, applications, its greatest strength was always in scripting and customizing applications. NetRexx supports these tasks equally well (indeed, some Rexx programs can be processed as NetRexx programs directly), and yet gains the scalability, power, and robustness of Java.

I had thought that programmers would always need two languages: one PL/I-like or C-like for high performance 'low level' programming, and one Rexx-like for prototyping, rapid development, and scripting. I now see that the future is rosier: designing a single language for these traditionally disparate uses is indeed possible. This truly makes programming easier than it was before.

NetRexx on the World Wide Web

Many NetRexx resources can be found on the World Wide Web, including on-line documentation, sample programs, and the NetRexx reference implementation. See: `http://www2.hursley.ibm.com/netrexx`

Acknowledgments

Much of NetRexx is based on earlier work, and I am indebted to the hundreds of people who contributed to the development of Rexx, Object Rexx, and Java.

In recent years I have gained many insights from the deliberations of the members of the X3J18 technical committee, which, under the remarkable chairmanship of Brian Marks, led to the 1996 ANSI Standard for Rexx. Many of the committee's suggestions are incorporated in NetRexx.

Equally important have been the comments and feedback from the pioneering users of NetRexx, and all those people who sent me comments on the language either directly or in the NetRexx mailing list or forum. I would especially like to thank Ian Brackenbury, Barry Feigenbaum, Davis Foulger, Norio Furukawa, Dion Gillard, Martin Lafaix, Max Marsiglietti, and Trevor Turton for their insightful comments and encouragement.

I also thank IBM; my appointment as an IBM Fellow made it possible to make NetRexx a reality in months, rather than years.

Finally, this book has relied on old but trusted technology for its creation: its GML markup was processed using macros originally written by Bob O'Hara, and formatted using SCRIPT/VS, the IBM Document Composition Facility. Geoff Bartlett provided critical advice on character sets and fonts.

Mike Cowlishaw

Part 1

Background

This is the first of the three parts of this book, the second being an overview and introduction to the NetRexx language, and the third being the definition of the language.

This introductory part has two sections:

1. The reason for, and the objectives of, the NetRexx language
2. The concepts underlying the language design.

SECTION 1: LANGUAGE OBJECTIVES

This book introduces a new programming language, called NetRexx, which is derived from both Rexx and Java. NetRexx is intended as a dialect of Rexx that can be as efficient and portable as languages such as Java, while preserving the low threshold to learning and the ease of use of the original Rexx language.

Features of Rexx

The Rexx programming language[1] was designed with just one objective: to make programming easier than it was before. The design achieved this by emphasizing readability and usability, with a minimum of special notations and restrictions. It was consciously designed to make life easier for its users, rather than for its implementers.

---

1 Cowlishaw, M. F., **The REXX Language** (second edition), ISBN 0-13-780651-5, Prentice-Hall, 1990.

One important feature of Rexx syntax is *keyword safety*. Programming languages invariably need to evolve over time as the needs and expectations of their users change, so this is an essential requirement for languages that are intended to be executed from source.

Keywords in Rexx are not globally reserved but are recognized only in context. This language attribute has allowed the language to be extended substantially over the years without invalidating existing programs. Even so, some areas of Rexx have proved difficult to extend – for example, keywords are reserved within instructions such as **do**. Therefore, the design for NetRexx takes the concept of keyword safety even further than in Rexx, and also improves extensibility in other areas.

The great strengths of Rexx are its human-oriented features, including

- simplicity
- coherent and uncluttered syntax
- comprehensive string handling
- case-insensitivity
- arbitrary precision decimal arithmetic.

Care has been taken to preserve these. Conversely, its unusually dynamic nature has always entailed a lack of efficiency: excellent Rexx compilers do exist, from IBM and other companies, but cannot offer the full speed of statically-scoped languages such as C[2] or Java.[3]

Influence of Java

The system-independent design of Rexx makes it an obvious and natural fit to a system-independent execution environment such as that provided by the Java Virtual Machine (JVM). The JVM, especially when enhanced with "just-in-time" bytecode compilers that compile bytecodes into native code just before execution, offers an effective and attractive target environment for a language like Rexx.

Choosing the JVM as a target environment does, however, place significant constraints on the design of a language suitable for that environment. For example, the semantics of method invocation are in several ways determined by the environment rather than by the source language, and, to a large extent, the object model (class structure, *etc.*) of the Java environment is imposed on languages that use it.

---

[2] Kernighan, B. W., and Ritchie, D. M., **The C Programming Language** (second edition), ISBN 0-13-110362-8, Prentice-Hall, 1988.

[3] Gosling, J. A., *et al.* **The Java Language Specification**, ISBN 0-201-63451-1, Addison-Wesley, 1996.

Also, Java maintains the C concept of primitive datatypes; types (such as `int`, a 32-bit signed integer) which allow efficient use of the underlying hardware yet do not describe true objects. These types are pervasive in classes and interfaces written in the Java language; any language intending to use Java classes effectively must provide access to these types.

Equally, the *exception* (error handling) model of Java is pervasive, to the extent that methods must check certain exceptions and declare those that are not handled within the method. This makes it difficult to fit an alternative exception model.

The constraints of safety, efficiency, and environment necessitated that NetRexx would have to differ in some details of syntax and semantics from Rexx; it could not be a fully upwards-compatible extension of the language, like Object Rexx.[4] The need for changes, however, offered the opportunity to make some significant simplifications and enhancements to the language, both to improve its keyword safety and to strengthen other features of the original Rexx design.[5] Some additions from Object Rexx and ANSI Rexx[6] are also included.

Similarly, the concepts and philosophy of the Rexx design can profitably be applied to avoid many of the minor irregularities that characterize the C and Java language family, by providing suitable simplifications in the programming model. For example, the NetRexx looping construct has only one form, rather than three, and exception handling can be applied to all blocks rather than requiring an extra construct. Also, as in Rexx, all NetRexx storage allocation and de-allocation is implicit – an explicit `new` operator is not required.

Further, the human-oriented design features of Rexx (case-insensitivity for identifiers, type deduction from context, automatic conversions where safe, tracing, and a strong emphasis on string representations of common values and numbers) make programming for the Java environment especially easy in NetRexx.

A hybrid or a whole?

As in other mixtures, not all blends are a success; when first designing NetRexx, it was not at all obvious whether the new language would be an

---

4 Nash, S. C., **Object-Oriented REXX** *in* Goldberg, G, and Smith, P. H. III, **The Rexx Handbook**, pp115-125, ISBN 0-07-023682-8, McGraw-Hill, Inc., New York, 1992.

5 See Cowlishaw, M. F., **The Early History of REXX**, *IEEE Annals of the History of Computing*, ISSN 1058-6180, Vol 16, No. 4, Winter 1994, pp15-24, and Cowlishaw, M. F., **The Future of Rexx**, *Proceedings of Winter 1993 Meeting/SHARE 80*, Volume II, p.2709, SHARE Inc., Chicago, 1993.

6 See **American National Standard for Information Technology – Programming Language REXX**, X3.274-1996, American National Standards Institute, New York, 1996.

improvement on its parents, or would simply reflect the worst features of both.

The fulcrum of the design is perhaps the way in which datatyping is automated without losing the static typing supported by Java. Typing in NetRexx is most apparent at interfaces – where it provides most value – but within methods it is subservient and does not obscure algorithms. A simple concept, *binary classes*, also lets the programmer choose between robust decimal arithmetic and less safe (but faster) binary arithmetic for advanced programming where performance is a primary consideration.

The "seamless" integration of types into what was previously an essentially typeless language does seem to have been a success, offering the advantages of strong typing while preserving the ease of use and speed of development that Rexx programmers have enjoyed.

The end result of adding Java typing capabilities to the Rexx language is a single new language that has both the Rexx strengths for scripting and for writing macros for applications and the Java strengths of robustness, good efficiency, portability, and security for application development.

SECTION 2: LANGUAGE CONCEPTS

As described in the last section, NetRexx was created by applying the philosophy of the Rexx language to the semantics required for programming the Java Virtual Machine (JVM). Despite the assumption that the JVM is a "target environment" for NetRexx, it is intended that the language not be environment-dependent; the essentials of the language do not depend on the JVM. Environment-dependent details, such as the primitive types supported, are not part of the language specification.

The primary concepts of Rexx have been described before, in *The Rexx Language*, but it is worth repeating them and also indicating where modifications and additions have been necessary to support the concepts of statically-typed and object-oriented environments. The remainder of this section is therefore a summary of the principal concepts of NetRexx.

Readability

One concept was central to the evolution of Rexx syntax, and hence NetRexx syntax: *readability* (used here in the sense of perceived legibility). Readability in this sense is a somewhat subjective quality, but the general principle followed is that the tokens which form a program can be written much as one might write them in Western European languages (English, French, and so forth). Although NetRexx is more formal than a natural language, its syntax is lexically similar to everyday text.

The structure of the syntax means that the language is readily adapted to a variety of programming styles and layouts. This helps satisfy user preferences and allows a lexical familiarity that also increases readability. Good readability leads to enhanced understandability, thus yielding fewer errors both while writing a program and while reading it for information, debugging, or maintenance. Important factors here are:

1. Punctuation and other special notations are required only when absolutely necessary to remove ambiguity (though punctuation may often be added according to personal preference, so long as it is syntactically correct). Where notations are used, they follow established conventions.
2. The language is essentially case-insensitive. A NetRexx programmer may choose a style of use of uppercase and lowercase letters that he or she finds most helpful (rather than a style chosen by some other programmer).
3. The classical constructs of structured and object-oriented programming are available in NetRexx, and can undoubtedly lead to programs that are easier to read than they might otherwise be. The simplicity and small number of constructs also make NetRexx an excellent language for teaching the concepts of good structure.
4. Loose binding between the physical lines in a program and the syntax of the language ensures that even though programs are affected by line ends, they are not irrevocably so. A clause may be spread over several lines or put on just one line; this flexibility helps a programmer lay out the program in the style felt to be most readable.

Natural data typing and decimal arithmetic

"Strong typing", in which the values that a variable may take are tightly constrained, has been an attribute of some languages for many years. The greatest advantage of strong typing is for the interfaces between program modules, where errors are easy to introduce and difficult to catch. Errors *within* modules that would be detected by strong typing (and which would not be detected from context) are much rarer, certainly when compared with design errors, and in the majority of cases do not justify the added program complexity.

NetRexx, therefore, treats types as unobtrusively as possible, with a simple syntax for type description which makes it easy to make types explicit at interfaces (for example, when describing the arguments to methods).

By default, common values (identifiers, numbers, and so on) are described in the form of the symbolic notation (strings of characters) that a user would normally write to represent those values. This natural datatype for values also supports decimal arithmetic for numbers, so, from the user's perspective, numbers look like and are manipulated as strings, just as they would be in everyday use on paper.

When dealing with values in this way, no internal or machine representation of characters or numbers is exposed in the language, and so the need for many data types is reduced. There are, for example, no fundamentally different concepts of *integer* and *real*; there is just the single concept of *number*. The results of all operations have a defined symbolic representation, and will therefore act consistently and predictably for every correct implementation.

This concept also underlies the BASIC[7] language; indeed, Kemeny and Kurtz's vision for BASIC included many of the fundamental principles that inspired Rexx. For example, Thomas E. Kurtz wrote:

> "Regarding variable types, we felt that a distinction between 'fixed' and 'floating' was less justified in 1964 than earlier ... to our potential audience the distinction between an integer number and a non-integer number would seem esoteric. A number is a number is a number."[8]

For Rexx, intended as a scripting language, this approach was ideal; symbolic operations were all that were necessary.

For NetRexx, however, it is recognized that for some applications it is necessary to take full advantage of the performance of the underlying environment, and so the language allows for the use and specification of binary arithmetic and types, if available. A very simple mechanism (declaring a class to be *binary*) is provided to indicate to the language processor that binary arithmetic and types are to be used where applicable. In this case, as in other languages, extra care has to be taken by the programmer to avoid exceeding limits of number size and so on.

Emphasis on symbolic manipulation

Many values that NetRexx manipulates are (from the user's point of view, at least) in the form of strings of characters. Productivity is greatly enhanced if these strings can be handled as easily as manipulating words on a page or in a text editor. NetRexx therefore has a rich set of character manipulation operators and methods, which operate on values of type `Rexx` (the name of the class of NetRexx strings).

Concatenation, the most common string operation, is treated specially in NetRexx. In addition to a conventional concatenate operator ("||"), the novel *blank operator* from Rexx concatenates two data strings together with a blank in between. Furthermore, if two syntactically distinct terms (such as a string and a variable name) are abutted, then the data strings are concatenated directly. These operators make it especially easy to build up complex character strings, and may at any time be combined with the other operators.

---

7 Kemeny, J. G. and Kurtz, T. E., **BASIC programming**, John Wiley & Sons Inc., New York, 1967.

8 Kurtz, T. E., **BASIC** *in* Wexelblat, R. L. (Ed), **History of Programming Languages**, ISBN 0-12-745040-8, Academic Press, New York 1981.

For example, the **say** instruction consists of the keyword **say** followed by any expression. In this instance of the instruction, if the variable n has the value "6" then

```
say 'Sorry,' n*100/50'% were rejected'
```

would display the string

```
Sorry, 12% were rejected
```

Concatenation has a lower priority than the arithmetic operators. The order of evaluation of the expression is therefore first the multiplication, then the division, then the concatenate-with-blank, and finally the direct concatenation.

Since the concatenation operators are distinct from the arithmetic operators, very natural coercion (automatic conversion) between numbers and character strings is possible. Further, explicit type-casting (conversion of types) is effected by the same operators, at the same priority, making for a very natural and consistent syntax for changing the types of results. For example,

```
i=int 100/7
```

would calculate the result of 100 divided by 7, convert that result to an integer (assuming int describes an integer type) and then assign it to the variable i.

Nothing to declare

Consistent with the philosophy of simplicity, NetRexx does not require that variables within methods be declared before use. Only the *properties*[9] of classes – which may form part of their interface to other classes – need be listed formally.

Within methods, the type of variables is deduced statically from context, which saves the programmer the menial task of stating the type explicitly. Of course, if preferred, variables may be listed and assigned a type at the start of each method.

Environment independence

The core NetRexx language is independent of both operating systems and hardware. NetRexx programs, though, must be able to interact with their environment, which implies some dependence on that environment (for example, binary representations of numbers may be required). Certain areas of the language are therefore described as being defined by the environment.

---

9 Class variables and instance variables.

Where environment-independence is defined, however, there may be a loss of efficiency – though this can usually be justified in view of the simplicity and portability gained.

As an example, character string comparison in NetRexx is normally independent of case and of leading and trailing blanks. (The string " Yes " *means* the same as "yes" in most applications.) However, the influence of underlying hardware has often subtly affected this kind of design decision, so that many languages only allow trailing blanks but not leading blanks, and insist on exact case matching. By contrast, NetRexx provides the human-oriented relaxed comparison for strings as default, with optional "strict comparison" operators.

Limited span syntactic units

The fundamental unit of syntax in the NetRexx language is the clause, which is a piece of program text terminated by a semicolon (usually implied by the end of a line). The span of syntactic units is therefore small, usually one line or less. This means that the syntax parser in the language processor can rapidly detect and locate errors, which in turn means that error messages can be both precise and concise.

It is difficult to provide good diagnostics for languages (such as Pascal and its derivatives) that have large fundamental syntactic units. For these languages, a small error can often have a major or distributed effect on the parser, which can lead to multiple error messages or even misleading error messages.

Dealing with reality

A computer language is a tool for use by real people to do real work. Any tool must, above all, be reliable. In the case of a language this means that it should do what the user expects. User expectations are generally based on prior experience, including the use of various programming and natural languages, and on the human ability to abstract and generalize.

It is difficult to define exactly how to meet user expectations, but it helps to ask the question "Could there be a high *astonishment factor* associated with this feature?". If a feature, accidentally misused, gives apparently unpredictable results, then it has a high astonishment factor and is therefore undesirable.

Another important attribute of a reliable software tool is *consistency*. A consistent language is by definition predictable and is often elegant. The danger here is to assume that because a rule is consistent and easily described, it is therefore simple to understand. Unfortunately, some of the most elegant rules can lead to effects that are completely alien to the intuition and expectations of a user who, after all, is human.

These constraints make programming language design more of an art than a science, if the usability of the language is a primary goal. The problems are further compounded for NetRexx because the language is suitable for both scripting (where rapid development and ease of use are paramount) and for application development (where some programmers prefer extensive checking and redundant coding). These conflicting goals are balanced in NetRexx by providing automatic handling of many tasks (such as conversions between different representations of strings and numbers) yet allowing for "strict" options which, for example, may require that all types be explicit, identifiers be identical in case as well as spelling, and so on.

Be adaptable

Wherever possible NetRexx allows for the extension of instructions and other language constructs, building on the experience gained with Rexx. For example, there is a useful set of common characters available for future extensions, since only a restricted set is used for the few special notations in the language.

Similarly, the rules for keyword recognition allow instructions to be added whenever required without compromising the integrity of existing programs. There are no reserved keywords in NetRexx; variable names chosen by a programmer always take precedence over recognition of keywords; this ensures that NetRexx programs may safely be executed, from source, at a time or place remote from their original writing.

A language needs to be adaptable because *it certainly will be used for applications not foreseen by the designer.* Like all programming languages, NetRexx may (indeed, probably will) prove inadequate for certain future applications; room for expansion and change is included to make the language more adaptable and robust.

Keep the language small

NetRexx is designed as a small language. It is not the sum of all the features of Rexx and of Java; rather, unnecessary features have been omitted. The intention has been to keep the language as small as possible, so that users can rapidly grasp most of the language. This means that:

- the language appears less formidable to the new user
- documentation is smaller and simpler
- the experienced user can be aware of all the abilities of the language, and so has the whole tool at his or her disposal
- there are few exceptions, special cases, or rarely used embellishments
- the language is easier to implement.

Many languages have accreted "neat" features which make certain algorithms easier to express; analysis shows that many of these are rarely used. As a rough rule-of-thumb, features that simply provided alternative ways of writing code were added to Rexx and NetRexx only if they were likely to be used more often than once in five thousand clauses.

No defined size or shape limits

The language does not define limits on the size or shape of any of its tokens or data (although there may be implementation restrictions). It does, however, define a few *minimum* requirements that must be satisfied by an implementation. Wherever an implementation restriction has to be applied, it is recommended that it should be of such a magnitude that few (if any) users will be affected.

Where arbitrary implementation limits are necessary, the language requires that the implementer use familiar and memorable decimal values for the limits. For example 250 would be used in preference to 255, 500 to 512, and so on.

Part 2

NetRexx Overview

This part of the book summarises the main features of NetRexx, and is intended to help you start using it quickly. It's assumed that you have some knowledge of programming in a language such as Rexx, C, BASIC, or Java, but a knowledge of "object-oriented" programming isn't needed.

This is not a complete tutorial, though – think of it more as a "taster"; it covers the main points of the language and shows some examples you can try or modify. For full details for the language, consult Part 3, the *NetRexx Language Definition* (see page 29).

SECTION 1: NETREXX PROGRAMS

The structure of a NetRexx program is extremely simple. This sample program, "toast", is complete, documented, and executable as it stands:

```
/* This wishes you the best of health. */
say 'Cheers!'
```

This program consists of two lines: the first is an optional comment that describes the purpose of the program, and the second is a **say** instruction. **say** simply displays the result of the expression following it – in this case just a literal string (you can use either single or double quotes around strings, as you prefer).

To run this program using the reference implementation of NetRexx, create a file called `toast.nrx` and copy or paste the two lines above into it. You can then use the `NetRexxC` Java program to compile it:

```
java netrexx.process.NetRexxC toast
```

(this should create a file called `toast.class`), and then use the `java` command to run it:

```
java toast
```

You may also be able to use the `netrexxc` or `nrc` command to compile and run the program with a single command (details may vary – see the installation and user's guide document for your implementation of NetRexx):

```
netrexxc toast -run
```

Of course, NetRexx can do more than just display a character string. Although the language has a simple syntax, and has a small number of instruction types, it is powerful; the reference implementation of the language allows full access to the rapidly growing collection of Java programs known as *class libraries*, and allows new class libraries to be written in NetRexx.

The rest of this overview introduces most of the features of NetRexx. Since the economy, power, and clarity of expression in NetRexx is best appreciated with use, you are urged to try using the language yourself.

SECTION 2: EXPRESSIONS AND VARIABLES

Like **say** in the "toast" example, many instructions in NetRexx include *expressions* that will be evaluated. NetRexx provides arithmetic operators (including integer division, remainder, and power operators), several concatenation operators, comparison operators, and logical operators. These can be used in any combination within a NetRexx expression (provided, of course, that the data values are valid for those operations).

All the operators act upon strings of characters (known as *NetRexx strings*), which may be of any length (typically limited only by the amount of storage available). Quotes (either single or double) are used to indicate literal strings, and are optional if the literal string is just a number. For example, the expressions:

```
'2' + '3'
'2' + 3
  2 + 3
```

would all result in `'5'`.

The results of expressions are often assigned to *variables*, using a conventional assignment syntax:

```
var1=5              /* sets var1 to '5'    */
var2=(var1+2)*10    /* sets var2 to '70' */
```

You can write the names of variables (and keywords) in whatever mixture of uppercase and lowercase that you prefer; the language is not case-sensitive.

This next sample program, "greet", shows expressions used in various ways:

```
/* greet.nrx -- a short program to greet you.          */
/* First display a prompt:                             */
say 'Please type your name and then press Enter:'
answer=ask            /* Get the reply into 'answer' */

/* If no name was entered, then use a fixed            */
/* greeting, otherwise echo the name politely.         */
if answer='' then say 'Hello Stranger!'
             else say 'Hello' answer'!'
```

After displaying a prompt, the program reads a line of text from the user ("ask" is a keyword provided by NetRexx) and assigns it to the variable answer. This is then tested to see if any characters were entered, and different actions are taken accordingly; for example, if the user typed "Fred" in response to the prompt, then the program would display:

```
Hello Fred!
```

As you see, the expression on the last **say** (display) instruction concatenated the string "Hello" to the value of variable answer with a blank in between them (the blank is here a valid operator, meaning "concatenate with blank"). The string "!" is then directly concatenated to the result built up so far. These unobtrusive operators (the *blank operator* and abuttal) for concatenation are very natural and easy to use, and make building text strings simple and clear.

The layout of instructions is very flexible. In the "greet" example, for instance, the **if** instruction could be laid out in a number of ways, according to personal preference. Line breaks can be added at either side of the **then** (or following the **else**).

In general, instructions are ended by the end of a line. To continue a instruction to a following line, you can use a hyphen (minus sign) just as in English:

```
say 'Here we have an expression that is quite long,' -
    'so it is split over two lines'
```

This acts as though the two lines were all on one line, with the hyphen and any blanks around it being replaced by a single blank. The net result is two strings concatenated together (with a blank in between) and then displayed.

When desired, multiple instructions can be placed on one line with the aid of the semicolon separator:

```
if answer='Yes' then do; say 'OK!'; exit; end
```

(many people find multiple instructions on one line hard to read, but sometimes it is convenient).

SECTION 3: CONTROL INSTRUCTIONS

NetRexx provides a selection of *control* instructions, whose form was chosen for readability and similarity to natural languages. The control instructions include **if... then... else** (as in the "greet" example) for simple conditional processing:

```
if ask='Yes' then say "You answered Yes"
             else say "You didn't answer Yes"
```

select... when... otherwise... end for selecting from a number of alternatives:

```
select
  when a>0 then say 'greater than zero'
  when a<0 then say 'less than zero'
  otherwise say 'zero'
  end
```

do... end for grouping:

```
if a>3 then do
  say 'A is greater than 3; it will be set to zero'
  a=0
  end
```

and **loop... end** for repetition:

```
/* repeat 10 times; I changes from 1 to 10 */
loop i=1 to 10
  say i
  end
```

The **loop** instruction can be used to step a variable **to** some limit, **by** some increment, **for** a specified number of iterations, and **while** or **until** some condition is satisfied. **loop forever** is also provided, and **loop over** can be used to work through a collection of variables.

Loop execution may be modified by **leave** and **iterate** instructions that significantly reduce the complexity of many programs.

SECTION 4: NETREXX ARITHMETIC

Character strings in NetRexx are commonly used for arithmetic (assuming, of course, that they represent numbers). The string representation of numbers can include integers, decimal notation, and exponential notation; they are all treated the same way. Here are a few:

```
'1234'
'12.03'
'-12'
'120e+7'
```

The arithmetic operations in NetRexx are designed for people rather than machines, so are decimal rather than binary, do not overflow at certain values, and follow the rules that people use for arithmetic. The operations are completely defined by the ANSI standard for Rexx, so correct implementations will always give the same results.

An unusual feature of NetRexx arithmetic is the **numeric** instruction: this may be used to select the *arbitrary precision* of calculations. You may calculate to whatever precision that you wish (for financial calculations, perhaps), limited only by available memory. For example:

```
numeric digits 50
say 1/7
```

which would display

```
0.14285714285714285714285714285714285714285714285714
```

The numeric precision can be set for an entire program, or be adjusted at will within the program. The **numeric** instruction can also be used to select the notation (*scientific* or *engineering*) used for numbers in exponential format.

NetRexx also provides simple access to the native binary arithmetic of computers. Using binary arithmetic offers many opportunities for errors, but is useful when performance is paramount. You select binary arithmetic by adding the instruction:

```
options binary
```

at the top of a NetRexx program. The language processor will then use binary arithmetic (see page 26) instead of NetRexx decimal arithmetic for calculations, throughout the program.

SECTION 5: DOING THINGS WITH STRINGS

A character string is the fundamental datatype of NetRexx, and so, as you might expect, NetRexx provides many useful routines for manipulating strings. These are based on the functions of Rexx, but use a syntax that is more like Java or other similar languages:

```
phrase='Now is the time for a party'
say phrase.word(7).pos('r')
```

The second line here can be read from left to right as:

> take the variable `phrase`, find the seventh word, and then find the position of the first "`r`" in that word.

This would display "`3`" in this case, because "`r`" is the third character in "`party`".

(In Rexx, the second line above would have been written using nested function calls:

```
say pos('r', word(phrase, 7))
```

which is not as easy to read; you have to follow the nesting and then backtrack from right to left to work out exactly what's going on.)

In the NetRexx syntax, at each point in the sequence of operations some routine is acting on the result of what has gone before. These routines are called *methods*, to make the distinction from functions (which act in isolation). NetRexx provides (as methods) most of the functions that were evolved for Rexx, including:

- changestr (change all occurrences of a substring to another)
- copies (make multiple copies of a string)
- lastpos (find rightmost occurrence)
- left and right (return leftmost/rightmost character(s))
- pos and wordpos (find the position of string or a word in a string)
- reverse (swap end-to-end)
- space (pad between words with fixed spacing)
- strip (remove leading and/or trailing white space)
- verify (check the contents of a string for selected characters)
- word, wordindex, wordlength, and words (work with words).

These and the others like them, and the parsing described in the next section, make it especially easy to process text with NetRexx.

SECTION 6: PARSING STRINGS

The previous section described some of the string-handling facilities available; NetRexx also provides string parsing, which is an easy way of breaking up strings of characters using simple pattern matching.

A **parse** instruction first specifies the string to be parsed, often taken simply from a variable. This is followed by a *template* which describes how the string is to be split up, and where the pieces are to be put.

Parsing into words

The simplest form of parsing template consists of a list of variable names. The string being parsed is split up into words (sequences of characters separated by blanks), and each word from the string is assigned (copied) to the next variable in turn, from left to right. The final variable is treated specially in that it will be assigned a copy of whatever is left of the original string and may therefore contain several words. For example, in:

```
parse 'This is a sentence.'    v1 v2 v3
```

the variable `v1` would be assigned the value "`This`", `v2` would be assigned the value "`is`", and `v3` would be assigned the value "`a sentence.`".

Literal patterns

A literal string may be used in a template as a pattern to split up the string. For example

```
parse 'To be, or not to be?'    w1 ',' w2 w3 w4
```

would cause the string to be scanned for the comma, and then split at that point; each section is then treated in just the same way as the whole string was in the previous example.

Thus, `w1` would be set to "`To be`", `w2` and `w3` would be assigned the values "`or`" and "`not`", and `w4` would be assigned the remainder: "`to be?`". Note that the pattern itself is not assigned to any variable.

The pattern may be specified as a variable, by putting the variable name in parentheses. The following instructions:

```
comma=','
parse 'To be, or not to be?'    w1 (comma) w2 w3 w4
```

therefore have the same effect as the previous example.

Positional patterns

The third kind of parsing mechanism is the numeric positional pattern. This allows strings to be parsed using column positions.

SECTION 7: INDEXED STRINGS

NetRexx provides indexed strings, adapted from the compound variables of Rexx. Indexed strings form a powerful "associative lookup", or *dictionary*, mechanism which can be used with a convenient and simple syntax.

NetRexx string variables can be referred to simply by name, or also by their name qualified by another string (the *index*). When an index is used, a value associated with that index is either set:

```
fred=0           -- initial value
fred[3]='abc'    -- indexed value
```

or retrieved:

```
say fred[3]      -- would say "abc"
```

in the latter case, the simple (initial) value of the variable is returned if the index has not been used to set a value. For example, the program:

```
bark='woof'
bark['pup']='yap'
bark['bulldog']='grrrrr'
say bark['pup'] bark['terrier'] bark['bulldog']
```

would display

```
yap woof grrrrr
```

Note that it is not necessary to use a number as the index; any expression may be used inside the brackets; the resulting string is used as the index. Multiple dimensions may be used, if required:

```
bark='woof'
bark['spaniel', 'brown']='ruff'
say bark['spaniel', 'brown'] bark['terrier']
```

which would display

```
ruff woof
```

Here's a more complex example using indexed strings, a test program with a function (called a *static method* in NetRexx) that removes all duplicate words from a string of words:

```
/* justonetest.nrx -- test the justone function.       */
say justone('to be or not to be')  /* simple testcase */
exit

/* This removes duplicate words from a string, and     */
/* shows the use of a variable (HADWORD) which is      */
/* indexed by arbitrary data (words).                  */
method justone(wordlist) static
  hadword=0            /* show all possible words as new */
  outlist=''               /* initialize the output list */
  loop while wordlist\=''  /* loop while we have data */
    /* split WORDLIST into first word and residue     */
    parse wordlist word wordlist
    if hadword[word] then iterate /* loop if had word */
    hadword[word]=1 /* remember we have had this word */
    outlist=outlist word   /* add word to output list */
    end
  return outlist            /* finally return the result */
```

Running this program would display just the four words "`to`", "`be`", "`or`", and "`not`".

SECTION 8: ARRAYS

NetRexx also supports fixed-size *arrays*. These are an ordered set of items, indexed by integers. To use an array, you first have to construct it; an individual item may then be selected by an index whose value must be in the range `0` through `n-1`, where `n` is the number of items in the array:

```
array=String[3]          -- make an array of three Strings
array[0]='String one'    -- set each array item
array[1]='Another string'
array[2]='foobar'
loop i=0 to 2            -- display the items
  say array[i]
  end
```

This example also shows NetRexx *line comments*; the sequence "`--`" (outside of literal strings or "`/*`" comments) indicates that the remainder of the line is not part of the program and is commentary.

SECTION 9: THINGS THAT AREN'T STRINGS

In all the examples so far, the data being manipulated (numbers, words, and so on) are expressed as a string of characters. Many things, however, can be expressed more easily in some other way, so NetRexx allows variables to refer to other collections of data, which are known as *objects*.

Objects are defined by a name that lets NetRexx determine the data and methods that are associated with the object. This name identifies the type of the object, and is usually called the *class* of the object.

For example, an object of class Oblong might represent an oblong to be manipulated and displayed. The oblong could be defined by two values: its width and its height. These values are called the *properties* of the Oblong class.

Most methods associated with an object perform operations on the object; for example a `size` method might be provided to change the size of an Oblong object. Other methods are used to construct objects (just as for arrays, an object must be constructed before it can be used). In NetRexx and Java, these *constructor* methods always have the same name as the class of object that they build ("Oblong", in this case).

Here's how an Oblong class might be written in NetRexx (by convention, this would be written in a file called `Oblong.nrx`; implementations often expect the name of the file to match the name of the class inside it):

```
/* Oblong.nrx -- simple oblong class */
class Oblong
  width        -- size (X dimension)
  height       -- size (Y dimension)

  /* Constructor method to make a new oblong */
  method Oblong(newwidth, newheight)
    -- when we get here, a new (uninitialized) object
    -- has been created.  Copy the parameters we have
    -- been given to the properties of the object:
    width=newwidth; height=newheight

  /* Change the size of an Oblong */
  method size(newwidth, newheight) returns Oblong
    width=newwidth; height=newheight
    return this   -- return the resized object

  /* Change the size of an Oblong, relatively */
  method relsize(relwidth, relheight)-
                 returns Oblong
    width=width+relwidth; height=height+relheight
    return this

  /* 'Print' what we know about the oblong */
  method print
    say 'Oblong' width 'x' height
```

To summarize:

1. A class is started by the **class** instruction, which names the class.
2. The **class** instruction is followed by a list of the properties of the object. These can be assigned initial values, if required.
3. The properties are followed by the methods of the object. Each method is introduced by a **method** instruction which names the method and describes the arguments that must be supplied to the method. The body of the method is ended by the next method instruction (or by the end of the file).

The `Oblong.nrx` file is compiled just like any other NetRexx program, and should create a *class file* called `Oblong.class`. Here's a program to try out the Oblong class:

```
/* tryOblong.nrx -- try the Oblong class */

first=Oblong(5,3)            -- make an oblong
first.print                  -- show it
first.relsize(1,1).print     -- enlarge and print again

second=Oblong(1,2)           -- make another oblong
second.print                 -- and print it
```

when `tryOblong.nrx` is compiled, you'll notice (if your compiler makes a cross-reference listing available) that the variables `first` and `second` have type `Oblong`. These variables refer to Oblongs, just as the variables in earlier examples referred to NetRexx strings.

Once a variable has been assigned a type, it can only refer to objects of that type. This helps avoid errors where a variable refers to an object that it wasn't meant to.

Programs are classes, too

It's worth pointing out, here, that all the example programs in this overview are in fact classes (you may have noticed that compiling them with the reference implementation creates *xxx*`.class` files, where *xxx* is the name of the source file). The environment underlying the implementation will allow a class to run as a stand-alone *application* if it has a static method called `main` which takes an array of strings as its argument.

If necessary (that is, if there is no class instruction) NetRexx automatically adds the necessary class and method instructions for a stand-alone application, and also an instruction to convert the array of strings (each of which holds one word from the command string) to a single NetRexx string.

The automatic additions can also be included explicitly; the "toast" example could therefore have been written:

```
/* This wishes you the best of health. */
class toast
  method main(argwords=String[]) static
    arg=Rexx(argwords)
    say 'Cheers!'
```

though in this program the argument string, `arg`, is not used.

SECTION 10: EXTENDING CLASSES

It's common, when dealing with objects, to take an existing class and extend it. One way to do this is to modify the source code of the original class – but this isn't always available, and with many different people modifying a class, classes could rapidly get over-complicated.

Languages that deal with objects, like NetRexx, therefore allow new classes of objects to be set up which are derived from existing classes. For example, if you wanted a different kind of Oblong in which the Oblong had a new property that would be used when printing the Oblong as a rectangle, you might define it thus:

```
/* charOblong.nrx -- an oblong class with character */
class charOblong extends Oblong
  printchar        -- the character for display

  /* Constructor to make a new oblong with character */
  method charOblong(newwidth, newheight, newprintchar)
    super(newwidth, newheight) -- make an oblong
    printchar=newprintchar     -- and set the character

  /* 'Print' the oblong */
  method print
    loop for this.height
      say printchar.copies(this.width)
      end
```

There are several things worth noting about this example:

1. The "`extends Oblong`" on the class instruction means that this class is an extension of the Oblong class. The properties and methods of the Oblong class are *inherited* by this class (that is, appear as though they were part of this class).

   Another common way of saying this is that "`charOblong`" is a *subclass* of "`Oblong`" (and "`Oblong`" is the *superclass* of "`charOblong`").

2. This class adds the `printchar` property to the properties already defined for Oblong.

3. The constructor for this class takes a width and height (just like Oblong) and adds a third argument to specify a print character. It first invokes the constructor of its superclass (Oblong) to build an Oblong, and finally sets the printchar for the new object.

4. The new charOblong object also prints differently, as a rectangle of characters, according to its dimension. The `print` method (as it has the same name and arguments – none – as that of the superclass) replaces (overrides) the `print` method of Oblong.

5. The other methods of Oblong are not overridden, and therefore can be used on charOblong objects.

The `charOblong.nrx` file is compiled just like `Oblong.nrx` was, and should create a file called `charOblong.class`. Here's a program to try it out:

```
/* trycharOblong.nrx -- try the charOblong class */

first=charOblong(5,3,'#')   -- make an oblong
first.print                 -- show it
first.relsize(1,1).print    -- enlarge and print again

second=charOblong(1,2,'*')  -- make another oblong
second.print                -- and print it
```

This should create the two charOblong objects, and print them out in a simple "character graphics" form. Note the use of the method `relsize` from Oblong to resize the charOblong object.

Optional arguments

All methods in NetRexx may have optional arguments (omitted from the right) if desired. For an argument to be optional, you must supply a default value. For example, if the charOblong constructor was to have a default value for `printchar`, its method instruction could have been written:

```
method charOblong(newwidth, newheight, newprintchar='X')
```

which indicates that if no third argument is supplied then `'X'` should be used. A program creating a charOblong could then simply write:

```
first=charOblong(5,3)        -- make an oblong
```

which would have exactly the same effect as if `'X'` were specified as the third argument.

SECTION 11: TRACING

NetRexx tracing is defined as part of the language. The flow of execution of programs may be traced, and this trace can be viewed as it occurs (or captured in a file). The trace can show each clause as it is executed, and optionally show the results of expressions, *etc.* For example, the program:

```
trace results
number=1/7
parse number before '.' after
say after'.'before
```

would result in the trace:

```
2 *=*   number=1/7
  >v> number "0.142857143"
3 *=*   parse number before '.' after
  >v> before "0"
  >v> after "142857143"
4 *=*   say after'.'before
  >>> "142857143.0"
```

where the lines marked with "*=*" are the instructions in the program, lines with ">v>" show results assigned to local variables, and lines with ">>>" show results of un-named expressions.

Further, **trace methods** lets you trace the use of all methods in a class, along with the values of the arguments passed to each method. Here's the result of adding `trace methods` to the Oblong class shown earlier and then running `tryOblong`:

```
  8 *=*     method Oblong(newwidth, newheight)
    >a> newwidth "5"
    >a> newheight "3"
 26 *=*     method print
Oblong 5 x 3
 20 *=*     method relsize(relwidth, relheight)-
 21 *-*                   returns Oblong
    >a> relwidth "1"
    >a> relheight "1"
 26 *=*     method print
Oblong 6 x 4
 10 *=*     method Oblong(newwidth, newheight)
    >a> newwidth "1"
    >a> newheight "2"
 26 *=*     method print
Oblong 1 x 2
```

where lines with ">a>" show the names and values of the arguments.

SECTION 12: BINARY TYPES AND CONVERSIONS

Most programming environments support the notion of fixed-precision "primitive" binary types, which correspond closely to the binary operations usually available at the hardware level in computers. For the reference implementation, these types are:

- *byte, short, int,* and *long* – signed integers that will fit in 8, 16, 32, or 64 bits respectively
- *float* and *double* – signed floating point numbers that will fit in 32 or 64 bits respectively.
- *char* – an unsigned 16-bit quantity, holding a Unicode character
- *boolean* – a 1-bit logical value, representing `0` or `1` ("false" or "true").

Objects of these types are handled specially by the implementation "under the covers" in order to achieve maximum efficiency; in particular, they cannot be constructed like other objects – their value is held directly. This distinction rarely matters to the NetRexx programmer: in the case of string literals an object is constructed automatically; in the case of an `int` literal, an object is not constructed.

Further, NetRexx automatically allows the conversion between the various forms of character strings in implementations[10] and the primitive types. The "golden rule" that is followed by NetRexx is that any automatic conversion which is applied must not lose information: either it can be determined before execution that the conversion is safe (as in `int` to `String`) or it will be detected at execution time if the conversion fails (as in `String` to `int`).

The automatic conversions greatly simplify the writing of programs; the exact type of numeric and string-like method arguments rarely needs to be a concern of the programmer.

For certain applications where early checking or performance override other considerations, the reference implementation of NetRexx provides options for different treatment of the primitive types:

1. **options strictassign** – ensures exact type matching for all assignments. No conversions (including those from shorter integers to longer ones) are applied. This option provides stricter type-checking than most other languages, and ensures that all types are an exact match.
2. **options binary** – uses implementation-dependent fixed precision arithmetic on binary types (also, literal numbers, for example, will be treated as binary, and local variables will be given "native" types such as `int` or `String`, where possible).

---

[10] In the reference implementation, these are `String`, `char`, `char[]` (an array of characters), and the NetRexx string type, `Rexx`.

Binary arithmetic currently gives better performance than NetRexx decimal arithmetic, but places the burden of avoiding overflows and loss of information on the programmer.

The options instruction (which may list more than one option) is placed before the first class instruction in a file; the **binary** keyword may also be used on a **class** instruction, to allow an individual class to use binary arithmetic.

Explicit type assignment

You may explicitly assign a type to an expression or variable:

```
i=int 3000000    -- 'i' is an 'int' with value 3000000
j=int 4000000    -- 'j' is an 'int' with value 4000000
k=int            -- 'k' is an 'int', with no initial value
say i*j          -- multiply and display the result
k=i*j            -- multiply and assign result to 'k'
```

This example also illustrates an important difference between **options nobinary** and **options binary**. With the former (the default) the **say** instruction would display "`1.20000000E+13`" and a conversion overflow would be reported when the same expression is assigned to the variable `k`.

With **options binary**, binary arithmetic would be used for the multiplications, and so no error would be detected; the **say** would display "`-138625024`" and the variable `k` takes the incorrect result.

Binary types in practice

In practice, explicit type assignment is only occasionally needed in NetRexx. Those conversions that are necessary for using existing classes (or those that use **options binary**) are generally automatic. For example, here is an "Applet" for use by Java-enabled browsers:

```
/* A simple graphics Applet */
class Rainbow extends Applet
  method paint(g=Graphics)  -- called to repaint window
    maxx=size.width-1
    maxy=size.height-1
    loop y=0 to maxy
      col=Color.getHSBColor(y/maxy, 1, 1) -- new colour
      g.setColor(col)                     -- set it
      g.drawRect(0, y, maxx, y)           -- fill slice
    end y
```

In this example, the variable `col` will have type `Color`, and the three arguments to the method `getHSBColor` will all automatically be converted to type `float`. As no overflows are possible in this example, **options binary** may be added to the top of the program with no other changes being necessary.

SECTION 13: EXCEPTION AND ERROR HANDLING

NetRexx doesn't have a **goto** instruction, but a **signal** instruction is provided for abnormal transfer of control, such as when something unusual occurs. Using **signal** raises an *exception*; all control instructions are then "unwound" until the exception is caught by a control instruction that specifies a suitable **catch** instruction for handling the exception.

Exceptions are also raised when various errors occur, such as attempting to divide a number by zero. For example:

```
say 'Please enter a number:'
number=ask
do
  say 'The reciprocal of' number 'is:' 1/number
catch Exception
  say 'Sorry, could not divide "'number'" into 1'
  say 'Please try again.'
end
```

Here, the **catch** instruction will catch any exception that is raised when the division is attempted (conversion error, divide by zero, *etc.*), and any instructions that follow it are then executed. If no exception is raised, the **catch** instruction (and any instructions that follow it) are ignored.

Any of the control instructions that end with **end** (**do**, **loop**, or **select**) may be modified with one or more **catch** instructions to handle exceptions.

Part 3

NetRexx Language Definition

This part of the book describes the NetRexx language, version 1.00.

The language is described first in terms of the characters from which it is composed and its low-level syntax, and then progressively through more complex constructions. Finally, special sections describe the semantics of the more complicated areas.

Some features of the language, such as **options** keywords and binary arithmetic, are implementation-dependent. Rather than leaving these important aspects entirely abstract, this description includes summaries of the treatment of such items in the *reference implementation* of NetRexx. The reference implementation is based on the Java environment and class libraries.

Paragraphs that refer to the reference implementation, and are therefore not strictly part of the language definition, are shown in italics, like this one.

SECTION 1: NOTATIONS

In this part of the book, various notations such as changes of font are used for clarity. Within the text, a sans-serif bold font is used to indicate **keywords**, and the same font is used in italic to indicate *technical terms*. An italic font is used to indicate a reference to a *technical term defined elsewhere* or a *word* in a syntax diagram that names a segment of syntax.

Similarly, in the syntax diagrams in this book, words (symbols) in a bold font also denote **keywords** or sub-keywords, and words (such as *expression*) in italics denote a token or collection of tokens defined elsewhere. The brackets [and] delimit optional (and possibly alternative) parts of the instructions, whereas the braces { and } indicate that one of a number of alternatives must be selected. An ellipsis (. . .) following a bracket indicates that the bracketed part of the clause may optionally be repeated.

Occasionally in syntax diagrams (for indexed references) brackets are "real" (that is, a bracket is required in the syntax; it is not marking an optional part). These brackets are enclosed in single quotes, thus: **'['** or **']'**.

Note that the keywords and sub-keywords in the syntax diagrams are not case-sensitive: the symbols "IF" "If" and "iF" would all match the keyword shown in a syntax diagram as **if**.

Note also that most of the clause delimiters (";") shown may usually be omitted as they will be implied by the end of a line.

Appendix A (see page 171) collects together the syntax diagrams for ease of reference.

SECTION 2: CHARACTERS AND ENCODINGS

In the definition of a programming language it is important to emphasise the distinction between a *character* and the *coded representation*[11] (encoding) of a character. The character "A", for example, is the first letter of the English (Latin) alphabet, and this meaning is independent of any specific coded representation of that character. Different coded character sets (such as, for example, the ASCII[12] and EBCDIC[13] codes) use quite different encodings for this character (decimal values 65 and 193, respectively).

Except where stated otherwise, this book uses characters to convey meaning and not to imply a specific character code (the exceptions are certain operations that specifically convert between characters and their representations). At no time is NetRexx concerned with the glyph (actual appearance) of a character.

Character Sets

Programming in the NetRexx language can be considered to involve the use of two character sets. The first is used for expressing the NetRexx program itself, and is the relatively small set of characters described in the next section. The second character set is the set of characters that can be used as character data by a particular implementation of a NetRexx language processor. This character set may be limited in size (sometimes to a limit of 256 different characters, which have a convenient 8-bit representation), or it may be much larger. The *Unicode*[14] character set, for example, allows for 65536 characters, each encoded in 16 bits.

Usually, most or all of the characters in the second (data) character set are also allowed within a NetRexx program, but only within commentary or immediate (literal) data.

The NetRexx language explicitly defines the first character set, in order that programs will be portable and understandable; at the same time it avoids restrictions due to the language itself on the character set used for data. However, where the language itself manipulates or inspects the data (as when carrying out arithmetic operations), there may be requirements on the data character set (for example, numbers can only be expressed if there are digit characters in the set).

---

11 These terms have the meanings as defined by the International Organization for Standardization, in ISO 2382 *Data processing – Vocabulary*.

12 American Standard Code for Information Interchange.

13 Extended Binary Coded Decimal Interchange Code.

14 *The Unicode Standard: Worldwide Character Encoding*, Version 1.0. Volume 1, ISBN 0-201-56788-1, 1991, and Volume 2, ISBN 0-201-60845-6 1992, Addison-Wesley, Reading, MA.

SECTION 3: STRUCTURE AND GENERAL SYNTAX

A NetRexx program is built up out of a series of *clauses* that are composed of: zero or more blanks (which are ignored); a sequence of tokens (described in this section); zero or more blanks (again ignored); and the delimiter ";" (semicolon) which may be implied by line-ends or certain keywords. Conceptually, each clause is scanned from left to right before execution and the tokens composing it are resolved.

Identifiers (known as symbols) and numbers are recognized at this stage, comments (described below) are removed, and multiple blanks (except within literal strings) are reduced to single blanks. Blanks adjacent to operator characters (see page 36) and special characters (see page 37) are also removed.

Blanks and White Space

Blanks (spaces) may be freely used in a program to improve appearance and layout, and most are ignored. Blanks, however, are usually significant

- within literal strings (see below)
- between two tokens that are not special characters (for example, between two symbols or keywords)
- between the two characters forming a comment delimiter
- immediately outside parentheses ("(" and ")") or brackets ("[" and "]").

For implementations that support tabulation (tab) and form feed characters, these characters outside of literal strings are treated as if they were a single blank; similarly, if the last character in a NetRexx program is the End-of-file character (EOF, encoded in ASCII as decimal 26), that character is ignored.

Comments

Commentary is included in a NetRexx program by means of *comments.* Two forms of comment notation are provided; *line comments* are ended by the end of the line on which they start, and *block comments* are typically used for more extensive commentary.

Line comments

A line comment is started by a sequence of two adjacent hyphens ("--"); all characters following that sequence up to the end of the line are then ignored by the NetRexx language processor.

Example:

```
i=j+7  -- this line comment follows an assignment
```

Block comments

A block comment is started by the sequence of characters "/*", and is ended by the same sequence reversed, "*/". Within these delimiters any characters are allowed (including quotes, which need not be paired). Block comments may be nested, which is to say that "/*" and "*/" must pair correctly. Block comments may be anywhere, and may be of any length. When a block comment is found, it is treated as though it were a blank (which may then be removed, if adjacent to a special character).

Example:

```
/* This is a valid block comment */
```

The two characters forming a comment delimiter ("/*" or "*/") must be adjacent (that is, they may not be separated by blanks or a line-end).

Note: It is recommended that NetRexx programs start with a block comment that describes the program. Not only is this good programming practice, but some implementations may use this to distinguish NetRexx programs from other languages.

Implementation minimum: Implementations should support nested block comments to a depth of at least 10. The length of a comment should not be restricted, in that it should be possible to "comment out" an entire program.

Tokens

The essential components of clauses are called *tokens*. These may be of any length, unless limited by implementation restrictions,[15] and are separated by blanks, comments, ends of lines, or by the nature of the tokens themselves.

The tokens are:

Literal strings

A sequence including any characters that can safely be represented in an implementation[16] and delimited by the single quote character (`'`) or the double-quote (`"`). Use `""` to include a `"` in a literal string delimited

---

15 Wherever arbitrary implementation restrictions are applied, the size of the restriction should be a number that is readily memorable in the decimal system; that is, one of 1, 25, or 5 multiplied by a power of ten. 500 is preferred to 512, the number 250 is more "natural" than 256, and so on. Limits expressed in digits should be a multiple of three.

16 Some implementations may not allow certain "control characters" in literal strings. These characters may be included in literal strings by using one of the escape sequences provided.

by ", and similarly use two single quotes to include a single quote in a literal string delimited by single quotes. A literal string is a constant and its contents will never be modified by NetRexx. Literal strings must be complete on a single line (this means that unmatched quotes may be detected on the line that they occur).

Any string with no characters (*i.e.*, a string of length 0) is called a *null string*.

Examples:

```
'Fred'
'Aÿ'
"Don't Panic!"
":x"
'You shouldn''t'      /* Same as "You shouldn't" */
''                    /* A null string */
```

Within literal strings, characters that cannot safely or easily be represented (for example "control characters") may be introduced using an *escape sequence*. An escape sequence starts with a *backslash* ("\"), which must then be followed immediately by one of the following (letters may be in either uppercase or lowercase):

t — the escape sequence represents a tabulation (tab) character

n — the escape sequence represents a new-line (line feed) character

r — the escape sequence represents a return (carriage return) character

f — the escape sequence represents a form-feed character

" — the escape sequence represents a double-quote character

' — the escape sequence represents a single-quote character

\ — the escape sequence represents a backslash character

\- — the escape sequence represents a "null" character (the character whose encoding equals zero), used to indicate continuation in a **say** instruction

0 — (zero) the escape sequence represents a "null" character (the character whose encoding equals zero); an alternative to `\-`

xhh — the escape sequence represents a character whose encoding is given by the two hexadecimal digits ("hh") following the "x". If the character encoding for the implementation requires more than two hexadecimal digits, they are padded with zero digits on the left.

uhhhh — the escape sequence represents a character whose encoding is given by the four hexadecimal digits ("hhhh") following the "u".

It is an error to use this escape if the character encoding for the implementation requires fewer than four hexadecimal digits.

Hexadecimal digits for use in the escape sequences above may be any decimal digit (0-9) or any of the first six alphabetic characters (a-f), in either lowercase or uppercase.

Examples:

```
'You shouldn\'t'     /* Same as "You shouldn't" */
'\x6d\u0066\x63'     /* In Unicode: 'mfc' */
'\\\u005C'           /* In Unicode, two backslashes */
```

Implementation minimum: Implementations should support literal strings of at least 100 characters. (But note that the length of string expression results, *etc.*, should have a much larger minimum, normally only limited by the amount of storage available.)

Symbols

Symbols are groups of characters selected from the Roman alphabet in uppercase or lowercase (A-Z, a-z), the arabic numerals (0-9), and underscore. Implementations may also allow other alphabetic and numeric characters in symbols to improve the readability of programs in languages other than English. These additional characters are known as *extra letters* and *extra digits*.[17]

Examples:

```
DanYrOgof
minx
Élan
Virtual3D
```

A symbol may include other characters only when the first character of the symbol is a digit (0-9 or an extra digit). In this case, it is a *numeric symbol* – it may include a period ("`.`") and it must have the syntax of a number. This may be *simple number*, which is a sequence of digits with at most one period (which may not be the final character of the sequence), or it may be a number expressed in *exponential notation.*

A number in exponential notation is a simple number followed immediately by the sequence "`E`" (or "`e`"), followed immediately by a sign ("+" or "–"),[18] followed immediately by one or more digits (which may not be followed by any other symbol characters).

17 It is expected that implementations of NetRexx will be based on Unicode or a similarly rich character set. However, portability to implementations with smaller character sets may be compromised when extra letters or extra digits are used in a program.

18 The sign in this context is part of the symbol; it is not an operator.

Examples:

```
1
1.3
12.007
17.3E-12
3e+12
0.03E+9
```

When *extra digits* are used in numeric symbols, they must represent values in the range zero through nine. When numeric symbols are used as numbers, any extra digits are first converted to the corresponding character in the range 0-9, and then the symbol follows the usual rules for numbers in NetRexx (that is, the most significant digit is on the left, *etc.*).

In the reference implementation, the extra letters are those characters (excluding A-Z, a-z, and underscore) that result in `1` *when tested with* `java.lang.Character.isLetter`. *Similarly, the extra digits are those characters (excluding 0-9) that result in* `1` *when tested with* `java.lang.Character.isDigit`.

The meaning of a symbol depends on the context in which it is used. For example, a symbol may be a constant (if a number), a keyword, the name of a variable, or identify some algorithm.

Implementation minimum: Implementations should support symbols of at least 50 characters. (But note that the length of its value, if it is a string variable, should have a much larger limit.)

Operator characters

The characters `+ - * / % | & = \ > <` are used (sometimes in combination) to indicate operations (see page 56) in expressions. A few of these are also used in parsing templates, and the equals sign is also used to indicate assignment. Blanks adjacent to operator characters are removed, so, for example, the sequences:

```
345>=123
345 >=123
345 >=  123
345 > =  123
```

are identical in meaning.

Some of these characters may not be available in all character sets, and if this is the case appropriate translations may be used.

Note: The sequences "`--`", "`/*`", and "`*/`" are comment delimiters, as described earlier. The sequences "`++`" and "`\\`" are not valid in NetRexx programs.

Special characters

The characters `. , ; ) ( ] [` together with the operator characters have special significance when found outside of literal strings, and constitute the set of *special characters.* They all act as token delimiters, and blanks adjacent to any of these (except the period) are removed, except that a blank adjacent to the outside of a parenthesis or bracket is only deleted if it is also adjacent to another special character (unless this is a parenthesis or bracket and the blank is outside it, too).

Some of these characters may not be available in all character sets, and if this is the case appropriate translations may be used.

To illustrate how a clause is composed out of tokens, consider this example:

```
'REPEAT'   B + 3;
```

This is composed of six tokens: a literal string, a blank operator (described later), a symbol (which is probably the name of a variable), an operator, a second symbol (a number), and a semicolon. The blanks between the "`B`" and the "`+`" and between the "`+`" and the "`3`" are removed. However one of the blanks between the `'REPEAT'` and the "`B`" remains as an operator. Thus the clause is treated as though written:

```
'REPEAT' B+3;
```

Implied semicolons and continuations

A semicolon (clause end) is implied at the end of each line, except if:

1. The line ends in the middle of a block comment, in which case the clause continues at the end of the block comment.
2. The last token was a hyphen. In this case the hyphen is functionally replaced by a blank, and hence acts as a *continuation character.*

This means that semicolons need only be included to separate multiple clauses on a single line.

Notes:

1. A comment is not a token, so therefore a comment may follow the continuation character on a line.
2. Semicolons are added automatically by NetRexx after certain instruction keywords when in the correct context. The keywords that may have this effect are **else**, **finally**, **otherwise**, **then**; they become complete clauses in their own right when this occurs. These special cases reduce program entry errors significantly.

The case of names and symbols

In general, NetRexx is a *case–insensitive* language. That is, the names of keywords, variables, and so on, will be recognized independently of the case used for each letter in a name; the name "`Swildon`" would match the name "`swilDon`".

NetRexx, however, uses names that may be visible outside the NetRexx program, and these may well be referenced by case-sensitive languages. Therefore, any name that has an external use (such as the name of a property, method, constructor, or class) has a defined spelling, in which each letter of the name has the case used for that letter when the name was first defined or used.

Similarly, the lookup of external names is both case-preserving and case-insensitive. If a class, method, or property is referenced by the name "`Foo`", for example, an exact-case match will first be tried at each point that a search is made. If this succeeds, the search for a matching name is complete. If it is does not succeed, a case-insensitive search in the same context is carried out, and if one item is found, then the search is complete. If more than one item matches then the reference is ambiguous, and an error is reported.

Implementations are encouraged to offer an option that requires that all name matches are exact (case-sensitive), for programmers or house-styles that prefer that approach to name matching.

SECTION 4: TYPES AND CLASSES

Programs written in the NetRexx language manipulate values, such as names, numbers, and other representations of data. All such values have an associated *type* (also known as a *signature*).

The type of a value is a descriptor which identifies the nature of the value and the operations that may be carried out on that value.

A type is normally defined by a *class*, which is a named collection of values (called *properties*) and procedures (called *methods*) for carrying out operations on the properties.

For example, a character string in NetRexx is usually of type `Rexx`, which will be implemented by the class called `Rexx`. The class `Rexx` defines the properties of the string (a sequence of characters) and the methods that work on strings. This type of string may be the subject of arithmetic operations as well as more conventional string operations such as concatenation, and so the methods implement string arithmetic as well as other string operations.

The names of types can further be qualified by the name of a *package* where the class is held. See the **package** instruction for details of packages; in summary, a package name is a sequence of one or more non-numeric symbols, separated by periods. Thus, if the `Rexx` class was part of the `netrexx.lang` package,[19] then its *qualified type* would be `netrexx.lang.Rexx`.

In general, only the class name need be specified to refer to a type. However, if a class of the same name exists in more than one known (imported) package, then the name should be qualified by the package name. That is, if the use of just the class name does not uniquely identify the class then the reference is ambiguous and an error is reported.

Primitive types

Implementations may optionally provide *primitive types* for efficiency. Primitive types are “built-in” types that are not necessarily implemented as classes. They typically represent concepts native to the underlying environment (such as 32-bit binary integer numbers) and may exhibit semantics that are different from other types. NetRexx, however, makes no syntax distinction in the names of primitive types, and assumes *binary constructors* (see page 144) exist for primitive values.

Primitive types are necessary when performance is an overriding consideration, and so this definition will assume that primitive types corresponding to the common binary number formats are available and will describe how they differ from other types, where appropriate.

---

19 *This is in fact where it may be found in the reference implementation.*

In the reference implementation, the names of the primitive types are:

```
boolean char byte short int long float double
```

where the first two describe a single-bit value and Unicode character respectively, and the remainder describe signed numbers of various formats. The main difference between these and other types is that the primitive types are not a subclass of `Object`*, so they cannot be assigned to a variable of type* `Object` *or passed to methods "by reference". To use them in this way, an object must be created to "wrap" them; Java provides classes for this (for example, the class* `Long`*).*

Dimensioned types

Another feature that is provided for efficiency is the concept of *dimensioned types*, which are types (normal or primitive) that have an associated dimension (in the sense of the dimensions of an array). Dimensioned values are described in detail in the section on *Arrays* (see page 71).

The dimension of a dimensioned type is represented in NetRexx programs by square brackets enclosing zero or more commas, where the dimension is given by the number of commas, plus one. A dimensioned type is distinct from the type of the same name but with no dimensions.

Examples:

```
Rexx
int
Rexx[]
int[,,]
```

The examples show a normal type, a primitive type, and a dimensioned version of each (of dimension 1 and 3 respectively). The latter type would result from constructing an array thus:

```
myarray=int[10,10,10]
```

That is, the dimension of the type matches the count of indexes defined for the array.

SECTION 5: TERMS

A *term* in NetRexx is a syntactic unit which describes some value (such as a literal string, a variable, or the result of some computation) that can be manipulated in a NetRexx program.

Terms may be either *simple* (consisting of a single element) or *compound* (consisting of more than one element, with a period and no other characters between each element).

Simple terms

A simple term may be:

- A *literal string* (see page 33) – a character string delimited by quotes, which is a constant.
- A *symbol* (see page 35). A symbol that does not begin with a digit identifies a variable, a value, or a type. One that does begin with a digit is a *numeric symbol*, which is a constant.
- A *method call* (see page 47), which is of the form

  symbol **(** [*expression* [, *expression*] ...] **)**

- An *indexed reference* (see page 70), which is of the form[20]

  symbol '[' [*expression* [, *expression*] ...] ']'

- A *sub–expression* (see page 62), which consists of any expression enclosed within a left and a right parenthesis.

Blanks are not permitted between the symbol in a method call and the "(", or between the symbol in an indexed reference and the "[".

Within simple terms, method calls with no arguments (that is, with no expressions between the parentheses) may be expressed without the parentheses provided that they refer to a method in the current class (or to a static method in a class *used* by the current class) and do not refer to a constructor (see page 51). An implementation may optionally provide a mechanism that disallows this parenthesis omission.

20 The notations '[' and ']' indicate square brackets appearing in the NetRexx program.

Compound terms

Compound terms may start with any simple term, and, in addition, may start with a qualified class name (see page 103) or a qualified constructor (see page 47). These last two both start with a package name (a sequence of non-numeric symbols separated by periods and ending in a period).

This first part of a compound term is known as the *stub* of the term.

Example stubs:

```
"A string"
Arca
12.10
paint(g)
indexedVar[i+1]
("A" "string")
java.lang.Math              -- qualified class name
netrexx.lang.Rexx(1)        -- qualified constructor
```

All stubs are syntactically valid terms (either simple or compound) and may optionally be followed by a *continuation*, which is one or more additional non-numeric symbols, method calls, or indexed references, separated from each other and from the stub by *connectors* which are periods.

Example compound terms:

```
"A rabbit".word(2).pos('b')
Fluffy.left(3)
12.10.max(j)
paint(g).picture
indexedVar[i+1].length
("A" "string").word(1)
java.lang.Math.PI
java.lang.Math.log(10)
```

Within compound terms, method calls with no arguments (that is, with no expressions between the parentheses) may be expressed without the parentheses provided that they do not refer to a constructor (see page 51). For example, the term:

```
Thread.currentThread().suspend()
```

could be written:

```
Thread.currentThread.suspend
```

An implementation may optionally provide a mechanism that disallows this parenthesis omission.

Evaluation of terms

Simple terms are evaluated as a whole, as described below. Compound terms are evaluated from left to right. First the stub is evaluated according to the rules detailed below. The type of the value of the stub then qualifies the next element of the term (if any) which is then evaluated (again, the exact rules are detailed below). This process is then repeated for each element in the term.

For instance, for the example above:

```
"A rabbit".word(2).pos('b')
```

the evaluation proceeds as follows:

1. The stub ("A rabbit") is evaluated, resulting in a string of type Rexx.
2. Because that string is of type Rexx, the Rexx class is then searched for the word method. This is then invoked on the string, with argument 2. In other words, the word method is invoked with the string "A rabbit" as its current context (the properties of the Rexx class when the method is invoked reflect that value).

   This returns a new string of type Rexx, "rabbit" (the second word in the original string).
3. In the same way as before, the pos method of the Rexx class is then invoked on the new string, with argument 'b'.

   This returns a new string of type Rexx, "3" (the position of the first "b" in the previous result).

This value, "3", is the final value of the term.

The remainder of this section gives the details of term evaluation; it is best skipped on first reading.

Simple term evaluation

All simple terms may also be used as stubs, and are evaluated in precisely the same way as stubs, as described below. For example, numeric symbols are evaluated as though they were enclosed in quotes; their value is a string of type Rexx.

In binary classes (see page 76), however, simple terms that are strings or numeric symbols are given an implementation-defined string or primitive type respectively, as described in the section on *Binary values and operations* (see page 142)

Stub evaluation

A term's stub is evaluated according to the following rules:

- If the stub is a literal string, its value is the string, of type `Rexx`, constructed from that literal.
- If the stub is a numeric symbol, its value is the string, of type `Rexx`, constructed from that literal (as though the literal were enclosed in quotes).
- If the stub is an unqualified method or constructor call, or a qualified constructor call, then its value and type is the result of invoking the method identified by the stub, as described in *Methods and Constructors* (see page 47).
- If the stub is a (non-numeric) symbol, then its value and type will be determined by whichever of the following is first found:
  1. A local variable or method argument within the current method, or a property in the current class.
  2. A method whose name matches the symbol, and takes no arguments, and that is not a constructor, in the current class.[21] If the stub is part of a compound symbol, then it may also be in a superclass, searching upwards from the current class.
  3. A static or constant property, or a static method,[22] whose name matches the symbol (and that takes no arguments, if a method) in a class listed in the **uses** phrase of the **class** instruction. Each class from the list is searched for a matching property or method, and then its superclasses are searched upwards from the class in the same way; this process is repeated for each of the classes, in the order specified in the list.
  4. One of the allowed special words described in *Special words and methods* (see page 118), such as `this` or `version`.
  5. The short name of a known class or primitive type (in which case the stub has no value, just a type).
- If the stub is an indexed reference, then its value and type will be determined by whichever of the following is first found:
  1. The symbol naming the reference is an undimensioned local variable or method argument within the current method, or a property in the current class, which has type `Rexx`. In this case, the reference is to an *indexed string* (see page 70); the expressions within

---

[21] Unless parenthesis omission is disallowed by an implementation option, such as **options strictargs**.

[22] Unless parenthesis omission is disallowed by an implementation option, such as **options strictargs**.

the brackets must be convertible to type `Rexx`, and the type of the result will be `Rexx`.

2. The symbol naming the reference is a dimensioned local variable or method argument within the current method, or a property in the current class. In this case, the reference is to an *array* (see page 71), and the expressions within the brackets must be convertible to whole numbers allowed for array indexes. The type of the result will have the type of the array, with dimensions reduced by the number of dimensions specified in the stub.

   For example, if the array `foo` was of type `Baa[,,,]` and the stub referred to `foo[1,2]`, then the result would be of type `Baa[,]`. It would have been an error for the stub to have specified more than four dimensions.

3. The symbol naming the reference is the name of a static or constant property in a class listed in the **uses** phrase of the **class** instruction. Each class from the list is searched in the same way as for symbols, above. The reference may be to an *indexed string* or an *array*, as for properties in the current class.

4. The symbol naming the reference is the name of a primitive type or the short name of a known class, and there are no expressions within the brackets (just optional commas). In this case, the stub describes a *dimensioned type* (see page 40).

5. The symbol naming the reference is the name of a primitive type or is the short name of a known class, and there are one or more expressions within the brackets. In this case, the reference is to an *array constructor* (see page 71); the expressions within the brackets must be convertible to non-negative whole numbers allowed for array indexes, and the value is an array of the specified type, dimensions, and size.

- If the stub is a sub-expression, then its value and type will be determined by evaluating the *expression* (see page 56) within the parentheses.
- If the stub starts with the name of a package, then it will either describe a qualified type (see page 39) or a qualified constructor (see page 51). Its type will be same in either case, and if a constructor then its value will be the value returned by the constructor.

If the stub is not followed by further segments, the final value and type of the term is the value and type of the stub.

Continuation evaluation

Each segment of a term's continuation is evaluated from left to right, according to the type of the evaluation of the term so far (the *continuation type*) and the syntax of the new segment:

- If the segment is a method call, then its value and type is the result of invoking the matching method in the class defining the continuation type (or a superclass or subclass of that class), as described in *Methods and Constructors* (see page 47). Note that method calls in term continuations cannot be constructors.

- If the stub is an indexed reference, then it will refer to a property in the class defining the continuation type (or a superclass of that class). That property will either be an undimensioned NetRexx string (type `Rexx`) or a dimensioned array. In either case, it is evaluated in the same way as an indexed reference found in the stub, except that it is not necessarily in the current class, cannot be an array constructor, and cannot result in a dimensioned type.

- If the segment is a symbol, then it refers to either a property or a method in the class defining the continuation type (or a superclass of that class).[23]

  The search for the property or method starts with the class defining the continuation type. If a property name matches, it is used; if not, a method of the same name and having no arguments (or only optional arguments) will match. If neither property nor method is found, then the same search is applied to each of the continuation class's superclasses in turn, starting with the class that it extends.

  As a convenient special case, if the property or method is not found, then if the segment is the final segment of the term and is the simple symbol `length` and the continuation type is a single-dimensioned array, then the segment evaluates to the size of the array. This will be a non-negative whole number of an appropriate primitive type (or of type `Rexx` if there is no appropriate type).

The final value and type of the term is the value and type determined by the evaluation of the last segment of the continuation.

[23] Unless parenthesis omission is disallowed by an implementation option, such as **options strictargs**, in which case it can only be a property.

SECTION 6: METHODS AND CONSTRUCTORS

Instructions in NetRexx are grouped into *methods*, which are named routines that always belong to (are part of) a *class*.

Methods are invoked by being referenced in a term (see page 41), which may be part of an expression or be a clause in its own right (a method call instruction). In either case, the syntax used for a method invocation is:

symbol **(** [*expression* [, *expression*] ...] **)**

The *symbol*, which must be non-numeric, is called the *name* of the method. It is important to note that the name of the method must be followed immediately by the "(", with **no** blank in between, or the construct will not be recognized as a method call (a *blank operator* would be assumed at that point instead).

The *expressions* (separated by commas) between the parentheses are called the *arguments* to the method. Each argument expression may include further method calls.

The argument expressions are evaluated in turn from left to right and the resulting values are then passed to the method (the procedure for locating the method is described below). The method then executes some algorithm (usually dependent on any arguments passed, though arguments are not mandatory) and will eventually return a value. This value is then included in the original expression just as though the entire method reference had been replaced by the name of a variable whose value is that returned data.

For example, the `substr` method is provided for strings of type `Rexx` and could be used as:

```
c='abcdefghijk'
a=c.substr(3,7)
/* would set A to "cdefghi" */
```

Here, the value of the variable `c` is a string (of type `Rexx`). The `substr` (substring) method of the `Rexx` class is then invoked, with arguments `3` and `7`, on the value referred to by `c`. That is, the the properties available to (the context of) the `substr` method are the properties constructed from the literal string `'abcdefghijk'`. The method returns the substring of the value, starting at the third character and of length seven characters.

A method may have a variable number of arguments: only those required need be specified. For example, `'ABCDEF'.substr(4)` would return the string `'DEF'`, as the `substr` method will assume that the remainder of the string is to be returned if no length is provided.

Method invocations that take no arguments may omit the (empty) parentheses in circumstances where this would not be ambiguous. See the section on *Terms* (see page 41) for details.

Implementation minimum: At least 10 argument expressions should be allowed in a method call.

Method call instructions

When a clause in a method consists of just a term, and the final part of the term is a method invocation, the clause is a *method call instruction*:

```
symbol([expression [, expression]... ]);
```

The method is being called as a subroutine of the current method, and any returned value is discarded. In this case (and in this case only), the method invoked need not return a value (that is, the **return** instruction that ends it need not specify an expression).[24]

A method call instruction that is the first instruction in a constructor (see below) can only invoke the special constructors `this` and `super`.

Method resolution (search order)

Method resolution in NetRexx proceeds as follows:

- If the method invocation is the first part (stub) of a term, then:
  1. The current class is searched for the method (see below for details of searching).
  2. If not found in the current class, then the superclasses of the current class are searched, starting with the class that the current class extends.
  3. If still not found, then the classes listed in the **uses** phrase of the **class** instruction are searched for the method, which in this case must be a static method (see page 95). Each class from the list is searched for the method, and then its superclasses are searched upwards from the class; this process is repeated for each of the classes, in the order specified in the list.
  4. If still not found, the method invocation must be a constructor (see below) and so the method name, which may be qualified by a package name, should match the name of a primitive type or a

---

[24] A method call instruction is equivalent to the **call** instruction of other languages, except that no keyword is required.

known class (type). The specified class is then searched for a constructor that matches the method invocation.

- If the method invocation is not the first part of the term, then the evaluation of the parts of the term to the left of the method invocation will have resulted in a value (or just a type), which will have a known type (the continuation type). Then:

  1. The class that defines the continuation type is searched for the method (see below for details of searching).

  2. If not found in that class, then the superclasses of that class are searched, starting with the class that that class extends.

  If the search did not find a method, an error is reported.

  If the search did find a method, that is the method which is invoked, except in one case:

  - If the evaluation so far has resulted in a value (an object), then that value may have a type which is a subclass of the continuation type. If, within that subclass, there is a method that exactly overrides (see page 50) the method that was found in the search, then the method in the subclass is invoked.

  This case occurs when an object is earlier assigned to a variable of a type which is a superclass of the type of the object. This type simplification hides the real type of the object from the language processor, though it can be determined when the program is executed.

Searching for a method in a class proceeds as follows:

1. Candidate methods in the class are selected. To be a candidate method:

   - the method must have the same name as the method invocation (independent of the case (see page 38) of the letters of the name)

   - the method must have the same number of arguments as the method invocation (or more arguments, provided that the remainder are shown as optional in the method definition)

   - it must be possible to assign the result of each argument expression to the type of the corresponding argument in the method definition (if strict type checking is in effect, the types must match exactly).

2. If there are no candidate methods then the search is complete; the method was not found.

3. If there is just one candidate method, that method is used; the search is complete.

4. If there is more than one candidate method, the sum of the costs of the conversions (see page 55) from the type of each argument expression to the type of the corresponding argument defined for the method is computed for each candidate method.

5. The costs of those candidates (if any) whose names match the method invocation exactly, including in case, are compared; if one has a lower cost than all others, that method is used and the search is complete.
6. The costs of all the candidates are compared; if one has a lower cost than all others, that method is used and the search is complete.
7. If there remain two or more candidates with the same minimum cost, the method invocation is ambiguous, and an error is reported.

Note: When a method is found in a class, superclasses of that class are not searched for methods, even though a lower-cost method may exist in a superclass.

Method overriding

A method is said to *exactly override* a method in another class if

1. the method in the other class has the same name as the current method
2. the method in the other class is not **private**
3. the other class is a superclass of the current class, or is a class that the current class implements (or is a superclass of one of those classes).
4. the number and type of the arguments of the method in the other class exactly match the number and type of the arguments of the current method (where subsets are also checked, if either method has optional arguments).

For example, the `Rexx` class includes a `substr` (see page 164) method, which takes from one to three strings of type `Rexx`. In the class:

```
class mystring extends Rexx
  method substr(n=Rexx, length=Rexx)
    return this.reverse.substr(n, length)

  method substr(n=int, length=int)
    return this.reverse.substr(Rexx n, Rexx length)
```

the first method exactly overrides the `substr` method in the `Rexx` class, but the second does not, because the types of the arguments do not match.

A method that exactly overrides a method is assumed to be an extension of the overridden method, to be used in the same way. For such a method, the following rules apply:

- It must return a value of the same type as the overridden method (or none, if the overridden method returns none).
- If the overridden method is **public** then it must also be **public**, otherwise it must be either **public** or **inheritable**.
- If the overridden method is **static** then it must also be **static**.

- If the overridden method is not **static** then it must not be **static**.
- If the underlying implementation checks exceptions (see page 145), only those checked exceptions that are signalled by the overridden method may be left uncaught in the current method.

Constructor methods

As described above, methods are usually invoked in the context of an existing value or type. A special kind of method, called a constructor method, is used to actually create a value of a given type (an object).

Constructor methods always have the same short name as the class in which they are found, and construct and return a value of the type defined by that class (sometimes known as an *instance* of that class). If the class is part of a package, then the constructor call may be qualified by the package name.

Example constructors:

```
File('Dan.yr.Ogof')
java.io.File('Speleogroup.letter')
Rexx('some words')
netrexx.lang.Rexx(1)
```

There will always be at least one constructor if values can be created for a class. NetRexx will add a default constructor that takes no arguments if no constructors are provided, unless the components of the class are all static or constant, or the class is an interface class.

All constructors follow the same rules as other methods, and in addition:

1. Constructor calls always include parentheses in the syntax, even if no arguments are supplied. This distinguishes them from a reference to the type of the same name.
2. Constructors must call a constructor of their superclass (the class they extend) before they carry out any initialization of their own This is so any initialization carried out by the superclass takes place, and at the appropriate moment. Only after this call is complete can they make any reference to the special words `this` or `super` (see page 118).

   Therefore, the first instruction in a constructor must be either a call to the superclass, using the special constructor `super()` (with optional arguments), or a call to to another constructor in the same class, using the special constructor `this()` (with optional arguments). In the latter case, eventually a constructor that explicitly calls `super()` will be invoked and the chain of local constructor calls ends.

   As a convenience, NetRexx will add a default call to `super()`, with no arguments, if the first instruction in a constructor is not a call to `this()` or `super()`.

3. The properties of a constructed value are initialized, in the order given in the program, after the call to `super()` (whether implicit or explicit).

4. By definition, constructors create a value (object) whose type is defined by the current class, and then return that value for use. Therefore, the **returns** keyword on the **method** instruction (see page 93) that introduces the constructor is optional (if given, the type specified must be that of the class). Similarly, the only possible forms of the **return** instruction used in a constructor are either "`return this;`", which returns the value that has just been constructed, or just "`return;`", in which case, the "`this`" is assumed (this form will be assumed at the end of a method, as usual, if necessary).

Here is an example of a class with two constructors, showing the use of `this()` and `super()`, and taking advantage of some of the assumptions:

```
class MyChars extends SomeClass

  properties private
    /* the data 'in' the object */
    value=char[]

  /* construct the object from a char array */
  method MyChars(array=char[])
    /* initialize superclass */
    super()
    value=array                    -- save the value

  /* construct the object from a String */
  method MyChars(s=String)
    /* convert to char[] and use the above */
    this(s.toCharArray())
```

Objects of type `MyChars` could then be created thus:

```
myvar=MyChars("From a string")
```

or by using an argument that has type `char[]`.

SECTION 7: TYPE CONVERSIONS

As described in the section on *Types and classes* (see page 39), all values that are manipulated in NetRexx have an associated type. On occasion, a value involved in some operation may have a different type than is needed, and in this case conversion of a value from one type to another is necessary.

NetRexx considerably simplifies the task of programming, without losing robustness, by making many such conversions automatic. It will automatically convert values providing that there is no loss of information caused by the automatic conversion (or if there is, an exception would be raised).

Conversions can also be made explicit by concatenating a type (see page 60) to a value and in this case less robust conversions (sometimes known as *casts*) may be effected. See below for details of the permitted automatic and explicit conversions.

Almost all conversions carry some risk of failure, or have a performance cost, and so it is expected that implementations will provide options to either report costly conversions or require that programmers make all conversions explicit.[25] Such options might be recommended for certain critical programming tasks, but are not necessary for general programming.

Permitted automatic conversions

In general, the semantics of a type is unknown, and so conversion (from a *source type* to a *target type*) is only possible in the following cases:

- The target type and the source type are identical (the trivial case).
- The target type is a superclass of the source type, or is an interface class implemented by the source type. This is called *type simplification*, and in this case the value is not altered, no information is lost, and an explicit conversion may be used later to revert the value to its original type.
- The source type has a dimension, and the target type is `Object`.
- The source type is `null` and the target type is not primitive.
- The target and source types have known semantics (that is, they are "well-known" to the implementation) and the conversion can be effected without loss of information (other than knowledge of the original type). These are called *well–known conversions.*

Necessarily, the well-known conversions are implementation-dependent, in that they depend on the standard classes for the implementation and on the primitive types supported (if any). Equally, it is this automatic conversion

---

[25] *In the reference implementation,* **options strictassign** *may be used to disallow automatic conversions.*

between strings and the primitive types of an implementation that offer the greatest simplifications of NetRexx programming.

For example, if the implementation supported an `int` binary type (perhaps a 32-bit integer) then this can safely be converted to a NetRexx string (of type `Rexx`). Hence a value of type `int` can be added to a number which is a NetRexx string (resulting in a NetRexx string) without concern over the difference in the types of the two terms used in the operation.

Conversely, converting a long integer to a shorter one without checking for truncation of significant digits could cause a loss of information and would not be permitted.

In the reference implementation, the semantics of each of the following types is known to the language processor (the first four are all string types*, and the remainder are known as* binary numbers*):*

- `netrexx.lang.Rexx` – *the NetRexx string class*
- `java.lang.String` – *the Java string class*
- `char` – *the Java primitive which represents a single character*
- `char[]` – *an array of* `chars`
- `boolean` – *a single-bit primitive*
- `byte, short, int, long,` – *signed integer primitives (8, 16, 32, or 64 bits)*
- `float, double` – *floating-point primitives (32 or 64 bits)*

Under the rules described above, the following well-known conversions are permitted:

- `Rexx` *to* `binary number, char[], String,` *or* `char`
- `String` *to* `binary number, char[], Rexx,` *or* `char`
- `char` *to* `binary number, char[], String,` *or* `Rexx`
- `char[]` *to* `binary number, Rexx, String,` *or* `char`
- `binary number` *to* `Rexx, String, char[],` *or* `char`
- `binary number` *to* `binary number` *(if no loss of information can take place – no sign, high order digits, decimal part, or exponent information would be lost)*

Notes:

1. *Some of the conversions can cause a run-time error (exception), as when a string represents a number that is too large for an* `int` *and a conversion to* `int` *is attempted, or when a string that does not contain exactly one character is converted to a* `char`*.*

2. *The* `boolean` *primitive is treated as a binary number that may only take the values 0 or 1. A boolean may therefore be converted to any binary*

number type, as well as any of the string (or `char`*) types, as the character "*`0`*" or "*`1`*". Similarly, any binary number or string can be converted to boolean (and must have a value of 0 or 1 for the conversion to succeed).*

3. *The* `char` *type is a single-character string (it is not a number that represents the encoding of the character).*

Permitted explicit conversions

Explicit conversions are permitted for all permitted automatic conversions and, in addition, when:

- The target type is a subclass of the source type, or implements the source type. This conversion will fail if the value being converted was not originally of the target type (or a subclass of the target type).
- Both the source and target types are primitive and (depending on the implementation), the conversion may fail or truncate information.
- The target type is `Rexx` or a well-known string type (all values have an explicit string representation).

Costs of conversions

All conversions are considered to have a cost, and, for permitted automatic conversions, these costs are used to select a method for execution when several possibilities arise, using the algorithm described in *Methods and Constructors* (see page 48).

For permitted automatic conversions, the cost of a conversion from a *source type* to a *target type* will range from zero through some arbitrary positive value, constrained by the following rules:

- The cost is zero only if the source and target types are the same, or if the source type is `null` and the target type is not primitive.
- Conversions from a given primitive source type to different primitive target types should have different costs. For example, conversion of an 8-bit number to a 64-bit number might cost more than conversion of a 8-bit number to a 32-bit number.
- Conversions that may require the creation of a new object cost more than those that can never require the creation of a new object.
- Conversions that may fail (raise an exception) cost more than those that may require the creation of an object but can never fail.

Within these constraints, exact costs are arbitrary, and (because they mostly involve implementation-dependent primitive types) are necessarily implementation-dependent. The intent is that the "best performance" method be selected when there is a possibility of more than one.

SECTION 8: EXPRESSIONS AND OPERATORS

Many clauses can include *expressions*. Expressions in NetRexx are a general mechanism for combining one or more data items in various ways to produce a result, usually different from the original data.

Expressions consist of one or more terms (see page 41), such as literal strings, symbols, method calls, or sub-expressions, and zero or more *operators* that denote operations to be carried out on terms. Most operators act on two terms, and there will be at least one of these *dyadic* operators between every pair of terms.[26] There are also *prefix* (monadic) operators, that act on the term that is immediately to the right of the operator. There may be one or more prefix operators to the left of any term, provided that adjacent prefix operators are different.

Evaluation of an expression is left to right, modified by parentheses and by operator precedence (see page 62) in the usual "algebraic" manner. Expressions are wholly evaluated, except when an error occurs during evaluation.

As each term is used in an expression, it is evaluated as appropriate and its value (and the type of that value) are determined.

The result of any operation is also a value, which may be a character string, a data object of some other type, or (in special circumstances) a binary representation of a character or number. The type of the result is well-defined, and depends on the types of any terms involved in an operation and the operation carried out. Consequently, the result of evaluating any expression is a value which has a known type.

Note that the NetRexx language imposes no restriction on the maximum size of results, but there will usually be some practical limitation dependent upon the amount of storage and other resources available during execution.

Operators

The operators in NetRexx are constructed from one or more operator characters (see page 36). Blanks (and comments) adjacent to operator characters have no effect on the operator, and so the operators constructed from more than one character may have embedded blanks and comments. In addition, blank characters, where they occur between tokens within expressions but are not adjacent to another operator, also act as an operator.

The operators may be subdivided into five groups: concatenation, arithmetic, comparative, logical, and type operators. The first four groups work with terms whose type is "well-known" (that is, strings, or known types that can

---

[26] One operator, direct concatenation, is implied if two terms abut (see page 57).

be be converted to strings without information loss). The operations in these groups are defined in terms of their operations on strings.

Concatenation

The concatenation operators are used to combine two strings to form one string by appending the second string to the right-hand end of the first string. The concatenation may occur with or without an intervening blank:

`(blank)`	Concatenate terms with one blank in between.
`||`	Concatenate without an intervening blank.
`(abuttal)`	Concatenate without an intervening blank.

Concatenation without a blank may be forced by using the `||` operator, but it is useful to remember that when two terms are adjacent and are not separated by an operator,[27] they will be concatenated in the same way. This is the *abuttal* operation. For example, if the variable `Total` had the value `'37.4'`, then `Total'%'` would evaluate to `'37.4%'`.

Values that are not strings are first converted to strings before concatenation.

Arithmetic

Character strings that are numbers (see page 61) may be combined using the arithmetic operators:

`+`	Add.
`-`	Subtract.
`*`	Multiply.
`/`	Divide.
`%`	Integer divide. Divide and return the integer part of the result.
`//`	Remainder. Divide and return the remainder (this is not modulo, as the result may be negative).
`**`	Power. Raise a number to a whole number power.
`Prefix -`	Same as the subtraction: "`0`-number".
`Prefix +`	Same as the addition: "`0`+number".

---

[27] This can occur when the terms are syntactically distinct (such as a literal string and a symbol).

The section on *Numbers and Arithmetic* (see page 130) describes numeric precision, the format of valid numbers, and the operation rules for arithmetic. Note that if an arithmetic result is shown in exponential notation, then it is likely that rounding has occurred.

In binary classes (see page 76), the arithmetic operators will use binary arithmetic if both terms involved have values which are binary numbers. The section on *Binary values and operations* (see page 142) describes binary arithmetic.

Comparative

The comparative operators compare two terms and return the value `'1'` if the result of the comparison is true, or `'0'` otherwise. Two sets of operators are defined: the *strict* comparisons and the *normal* comparisons.

The strict comparative operators all have one of the characters defining the operator doubled. The "`==`", and "`\==`" operators test for strict equality or inequality between two strings. Two strings must be identical to be considered strictly equal. Similarly, the other strict comparative operators (such as "`>>`" or "`<<`") carry out a simple left-to-right character-by-character comparison, with no padding of either of the strings being compared. If one string is shorter than, and is a leading sub-string of, another then it is smaller (less than) the other. Strict comparison operations are case sensitive, and the exact collating order may depend on the character set used for the implementation.[28]

For all the other comparative operators, if **both** the terms involved are numeric,[29] a numeric comparison (in which leading zeros are ignored, *etc.*) is effected; otherwise, both terms are treated as character strings. For this character string comparison, leading and trailing blanks are ignored, and then the shorter string is padded with blanks on the right. The character comparison operation takes place from left to right, and is **not** case sensitive (that is, "`Yes`" compares equal to "`yes`"). As for strict comparisons, the exact collating order may depend on the character set used for the implementation.

The comparative operators return true (`'1'`) if the terms are:

Normal comparative operators:

`=`	Equal (numerically or when padded, *etc.*).
`\=`	Not equal (inverse of =).
`>`	Greater than.

---

28 For example, in an ASCII or Unicode environment, the digits 0-9 are lower than the alphabetics, and lowercase alphabetics are higher than uppercase alphabetics. In an EBCDIC environment, lowercase alphabetics precede uppercase, but the digits are higher than all the alphabetics.

29 That is, if they can be compared numerically without error.

`<` Less than.

`><, <>` Greater than or less than (same as “Not equal”).

`>=, \<` Greater than or equal to, not less than.

`<=, \>` Less than or equal to, not greater than.

Strict comparative operators:

`==` Strictly equal (identical).

`\==` Strictly not equal (inverse of `==`).

`>>` Strictly greater than.

`<<` Strictly less than.

`>>=, \<<` Strictly greater than or equal to, strictly not less than.

`<<=, \>>` Strictly less than or equal to, strictly not greater than.

The equal and not equal operators (“`=`”, “`==`”, “`\=`”, and “`\==`”) may be used to compare two objects which are not strings for equality, if the implementation allows them to be compared (usually they will need to be of the same type). The strict operators test whether the two objects are in fact the same object,[30] and the normal operators may provide a more relaxed comparison, if available to the implementation.[31]

In binary classes (see page 76), all the comparative operators will use binary arithmetic to effect the comparison if both terms involved have values which are binary numbers. In this case, there is no distinction between the strict and the normal comparative operators. The section on *Binary values and operations* (see page 142) describes the binary arithmetic used for comparisons.

Logical (Boolean)

A character string is taken to have the value “false” if it is `'0'`, and “true” if it is `'1'`. The logical operators take one or two such values (values other than `'0'` or `'1'` are not allowed) and return `'0'` or `'1'` as appropriate:

`&` And.
Returns 1 if both terms are true.

`|` Inclusive or.
Returns 1 if either term is true.

---

30 Note that two distinct objects compared in this way may contain values (properties) that are identical, yet they will not compare equal as they are not the same object.

31 *In the reference implementation, the* `equals` *method is used for normal comparisons. Where not provided by a type, this is implemented by the Object class as a strict comparison.*

`&&` Exclusive or.
Returns 1 if either (but not both) is true.

`Prefix \` Logical not.
Negates; 1 becomes 0 and *vice versa*.

In binary classes (see page 76), the logical operators will act on all bits in the values if both terms involved have values which are boolean or integers. The section on *Binary values and operations* (see page 142) describes this in more detail.

Type

Several of the operators already described can be used to carry out operations related to types. Specifically:

- Any of the concatenation operators may be used for *type concatenation*, which concatenates a type to a value. All three operators (blank, "||", and abuttal) have the same effect, which is to convert (see page 53) the value to the type specified (if the conversion is not possible, an error is reported or an exception is signalled). The type must be on the left-hand side of the operator.

  Examples:

  ```
  String "abc"
  int (a+1)
  long 1
  Exception e
  InputStream myfile
  ```

- The "less than or equal" and the "greater than or equal" operators ("<=" and ">=") may be used with a type on either side of the operator, or on both sides. In this case, they test whether a value or type is a subclass of, or is the same as, a type, or vice versa.

  Examples:

  ```
  if i<=Object then say 'I is an Object'
  if String>=i then say 'I is a String'
  if String<=Object then say 'String is an Object'
  ```

The precedence of these operators is not affected by their being used with types as operands.

Numbers

The arithmetic operators above require that both terms involved be numbers; similarly some of the comparative operators carry out a numeric comparison if both terms are numbers.

Numbers are introduced and defined in detail in the section on *Numbers and arithmetic* (see page 130). In summary, *numbers* are character strings consisting of one or more decimal digits optionally prefixed by a plus or minus sign, and optionally including a single period ("`.`") which then represents a decimal point. A number may also have a power of ten suffixed in conventional exponential notation: an "`E`" (uppercase or lowercase) followed by a plus or minus sign then followed by one or more decimal digits defining the power of ten.

Numbers may have leading blanks (before and/or after the sign, if any) and may have trailing blanks. Blanks may not be embedded among the digits of a number or in the exponential part.

Examples:

```
'12'
'-17.9'
'127.0650'
'73e+128'
' + 7.9E5 '
'0E000'
```

Note that the sequence `-17.9` (without quotes) in an expression is not simply a number. It is a minus operator (which may be prefix minus if there is no term to the left of it) followed by a positive number. The result of the operation will be a number.

A *whole number* (see page 139) in NetRexx is a number that has a zero (or no) decimal part.

Implementation minimum: All implementations must support 9-digit arithmetic. In unavoidable cases this may be limited to integers only, and in this case the divide operator ("`/`") must not be supported. If exponents are supported in an implementation, then they must be supported for exponents whose absolute value is at least as large as the largest number that can be expressed as an exact integer in default precision, *i.e.*, 999999999.

Parentheses and operator precedence

Expression evaluation is from left to right; this is modified by parentheses and by operator precedence:

- When parentheses are encountered, other than those that identify method calls (see page 47), the entire *sub–expression* delimited by the parentheses is evaluated immediately when the term is required.
- When the sequence

  $term_1$ $operator_1$ $term_2$ $operator_2$ $term_3$

  is encountered, and $operator_2$ has a higher precedence than $operator_1$, then the operation ($term_2$ $operator_2$ $term_3$) is evaluated first. The same rule is applied repeatedly as necessary.

  Note, however, that individual terms are evaluated from left to right in the expression (that is, as soon as they are encountered). It is only the order of **operations** that is affected by the precedence rules.

For example, "*" (multiply) has a higher precedence than "+" (add), so `3+2*5` will evaluate to 13 (rather than the 25 that would result if strict left to right evaluation occurred). To force the addition to be performed before the multiplication the expression would be written `(3+2)*5`, where the first three tokens have been formed into a sub-expression by the addition of parentheses.

The order of precedence of the operators is (highest at the top):

Prefix operators

```
+   -   \
```

Power operator

```
**
```

Multiplication and division

```
*   /   %   //
```

Addition and subtraction

```
+   -
```

Concatenation

```
(blank)   ||   (abuttal)
```

Comparative operators

`=   ==   >   <   <=  >=   <<   \>>` *etc.*

And

```
&
```

Or, exclusive or

```
|  &&
```

If, for example, the symbol a is a variable whose value is '3', and day is a variable with the value 'Monday', then:

```
a+5                ==   '8'
a-4*2              ==   '-5'
a/2                ==   '1.5'
a%2                ==   '1'
0.5**2             ==   '0.25'
(a+1)>7            ==   '0'                /* that is, False */
' '=''             ==   '1'                /* that is, True  */
' '==''            ==   '0'                /* that is, False */
' '\==''           ==   '1'                /* that is, True  */
(a+1)*3=12         ==   '1'                /* that is, True  */
'077'>'11'         ==   '1'                /* that is, True  */
'077'>>'11'        ==   '0'                /* that is, False */
'abc'>>'ab'        ==   '1'                /* that is, True  */
'If it is' day     ==   'If it is Monday'
day.substr(2,3)    ==   'ond'
'!'day'!'          ==   '!Monday!'
```

Note: The NetRexx order of precedence usually causes no difficulty, as it is the same as in conventional algebra and other computer languages. There are two differences from some common notations; the prefix minus operator always has a higher priority than the power operator, and power operators (like other operators) are evaluated left-to-right. Thus

```
-3**2       ==  9     /* not -9   */
-(2+1)**2   ==  9     /* not -9   */
2**2**3     ==  64    /* not 256 */
```

These rules were found to match the expectations of the majority of users when the Rexx language was first designed, and NetRexx follows the same rules.

SECTION 9: CLAUSES AND INSTRUCTIONS

Clauses (see page 32) are recognized, and can usefully be classified, in the following order:

Null clauses

A clause that is empty or comprises only blanks, comments, and continuations is a *null clause* and is completely ignored by NetRexx (except that if it includes a comment it will be traced, if reached during execution).

Note: A null clause is not an instruction, so (for example) putting an extra semicolon after the **then** or **else** in an **if** instruction is not equivalent to putting a dummy instruction (as it would be in C or PL/I). The **nop** instruction is provided for this purpose.

Assignments

Single clauses within a class and of the form *term=expression;* are instructions known as *assignments* (see page 65). An assignment gives a variable, identified by the *term*, a type or a new value.

In just one context, where property assignments are expected (before the first method in a class), the "=" and the expression may be omitted; in this case, the term (and hence the entire clause) will always be a simple non-numeric symbol which names the property

Method call instructions

A method call instruction (see page 48) is a clause within a method that comprises a single term that is, or ends in, a method invocation.

Keyword instructions

A *keyword instruction* consists of one or more clauses, the first of which starts with a non-numeric symbol which is not the name of a variable or property in the current class (if any) and is immediately followed by a blank, a semicolon (which may be implied by the end of a line), a literal string, or a operator (other than "=", which would imply an assignment). This symbol, the *keyword*, identifies the instruction.

Keyword instructions control the external interfaces, the flow of control, and so on. Some keyword instructions (see page 73) (**do**, **if**, **loop**, or **select**) can include nested instructions.

SECTION 10: ASSIGNMENTS AND VARIABLES

A *variable* is a named item whose value may be changed during the course of execution of a NetRexx program. The process of changing the value of a variable is called *assigning* a new value to it.

Each variable has an associated type, which cannot change during the execution of a program; therefore, the values assigned to a given variable must always have a type that can safely be assigned to that variable.

Variables may be assigned a new value by the **method** or **parse** instructions, but the most common way of changing the value of a variable is by using an *assignment instruction.* Any clause within a class and of the form:

> *assignment* ;
>
> where *assignment* is:
>
> *term* = *expression*

is taken to be an assignment instruction. The result of the *expression* becomes the new value of the variable named by the *term* to the left of the equals sign. When the term is simply a symbol, this is called the *name* of the variable.

Example:

```
/* Next line gives FRED the value 'Frederic' */
fred='Frederic'
```

The symbol naming the variable cannot begin with a digit (0-9).[32]

Within a NetRexx program, variable names are not case-sensitive (for example, the names `fred`, `Fred`, and `FRED` refer to the same variable). Where public names are exposed (for example, the names of properties, classes, and methods, and in cross-reference listings) the case used for the name will be that used when the name was first introduced ("first" is determined statically by position in a program rather than dynamically).

Similarly, the type of a NetRexx variable is determined by the type of the value of the expression that is first assigned to it.[33] For subsequent assignments, it is an error to assign a value to a variable with a type mismatch

---

32 Without this restriction on the first character of a variable name, it would be possible to redefine a number, in that for example the assignment "`3=4;`" would give a variable called "`3`" the value `'4'`.

33 Since NetRexx infers the type of a variable from usage, substantial programs can be written without introducing explicit type declarations, although these are allowed.

unless the language processor can determine that the value can be assigned safely to the type of the variable.

In practice, this means that the types must match exactly, be a simplification, or both be "well-known" types such as Rexx, String, int, *etc.*, for which safe conversions are defined. The possibilities are described in the section on *Conversions* (see page 53).[34]

For example, if there are types (classes) called ibm.util.hex, RunKnown, and Window, then:

```
hexy=ibm.util.hex(3) -- 'hexy' has type 'ibm.util.hex'
rk=RunKnown()        -- 'rk' has type 'RunKnown'
fred=Window(10, 20)  -- 'fred' has type 'Window'
s="Los Lagos"        -- 's' has type 'Rexx'
j=5                  -- 'j' has type 'Rexx'
```

The first three examples invoke the *constructor* method for the type to construct a value (an object). A constructor method always has the same name as the class to which it belongs, and returns a new value of that type. Constructor methods are described in detail in *Methods and Constructors* (see page 47).

The last two examples above illustrate that, by default, the types of literal strings and numbers are NetRexx strings (type Rexx) and so variables tend to be of type Rexx. This simplifies the language and makes it easy to learn, as many useful programs can be written solely using the powerful Rexx type. Potentially more efficient (though less human-oriented) primitive or built-in types for literals will be used in binary classes (see page 76).

If the examples above were in a binary class, then, in the reference implementation, the types of s *and* j *would have been* java.lang.String *and* int *respectively.*

A variable may be introduced ("declared") without giving it an initial value by simply assigning a type to it:

```
i=int
r=Rexx
f=java.io.File
```

Here, the expression to the right of the "=" simply evaluates to a type with no value.

---

[34] Implementations may provide for a stricter rule for assignment (where the types must be identical), controlled by the **options** instruction.

The use and scope of variables

NetRexx variables all follow the same rules of assignment, but are used in different contexts. These are:

Properties

Variables which name the values (the data) owned by an object of the type defined by the class are called *properties*. When an object is constructed by the class, its properties are created and are initialized to either a default value (`null` or, for variables of primitive type, an implementation-defined value, typically 0) or to a value provided by the programmer.

The attributes of properties can be changed by the **properties** instruction (see page 105). For example, properties may also be *constant*, which means that they are initialized when the class is first loaded and do not change thereafter.

Method arguments

When a method is invoked, arguments may be passed to it. These *method arguments* are assigned to the variables named on the **method** instruction (see page 93) that introduces the method.

Local variables

Variables that are known only within a method are called *local variables*; each time a method is invoked a distinct set of local variables is available. Local variables are normally given an initial value by the programmer. If they are not, they are initialized to a default value (`null` or, for variables of primitive type, an implementation-defined value, typically 0).

In order for types to be determined and type-checking to be possible at "compile-time", and easily determined by inspection, the use and type of every variable is determined by its position in the program, not by the order in which assignments are executed. That is, variable typing is static.

The visibility of a variable depends on its use. Properties are visible to all methods in a class; method arguments and local variables are only visible within the method in which they appear. In particular:

- Within a class, properties have unique names (they cannot be overridden by method arguments or by local variables within methods); this avoids error-prone ambiguity.
- Within a method, a method argument acts like a local variable (that is, it is in the same name-space as local variables, and can be assigned new values); it can be considered to be a local variable that is assigned a value just before the body of the method is executed. There cannot be both a method argument and a local variable in a method with the same name.

- Within methods, variables can take only one type, the type assigned to them when first encountered in the method (in a strict "physical" sense, that is, as parsed from top to bottom of the program and from left to right on each line). Since methods tend to be small, there is no local scoping of variables inside the constructs within a method.[35]

  Thus, in this example:

  ```
  method iszero(x)
    if x=0 then qualifier='is zero'
           else qualifier='is not zero'
    say 'The argument' qualifier'.'
  ```

  the variable `qualifier` is known throughout the method and hence has a known type and value when the **say** instruction is executed.

To summarize: a symbol that names a variable in the current class either refers to a property (and in any use of it within the class refers to that property), or it refers to a variable that is unique within a method (and any use of the name within that method refers to the same variable).

Note: A variable is just a name, or "handle" for a value. It is possible for more than one variable to refer to the same value, as in the program:

```
first='A string'
second=first
```

Here, both variables refer to the same value. If that value is changeable then a change to the value referred to by one of the variable names would also be seen if the value is referred to by the other. For example, sub-values of a NetRexx string can be changed, using *Indexed references* (see page 70), so a change to a sub-value of `first` would also be seen in an identical indexed reference to `second`.

Terms on the left of assignments

In an assignment instruction, the *term* to the left of the equals sign is most commonly a simple non-numeric symbol, which always names a variable in the current class. The other possibilities, as seen in the example below, are:

1. The term is an *indexed reference* (see page 70), to an existing variable that refers to a string of type `Rexx` or an array (see page 71). The variable may be in the current class, or be a property in a class named in the **uses** phrase of the **class** instruction for the current class.
2. The term is a compound term (see page 42) that ultimately refers to a property (see above) in some class (which may be the current class). This property cannot be a constant.

---

[35] Unlike the block scoping of PL/I, C, or Java.

Examples:

```
r=Rexx ''
r['foo']='?'           -- indexed string assignment
s=String[3]
s[0]='test'            -- array assignment
Sample.value=1         -- property assignment
this.value=1           -- property assignment
super.value=1          -- property assignment
```

The last two examples show assignments to a property in the current class or in a superclass of the current class, respectively. Note that references to properties in other classes must alway be qualified in some way (for example, by the prefix `super.`). The use of the prefix `this.` for properties in the current class is optional.

SECTION 11: INDEXED STRINGS AND ARRAYS

Any NetRexx string (that is, a value of type `Rexx`), has the ability to have *sub–values*, values (also of type `Rexx`) which are associated with the original string and are indexed by an *index string* which identifies the sub-value. Any string with such sub-values is known as an *indexed string*.

The sub-values of a NetRexx string are accessed using *indexed references*, where the name of a variable of type `Rexx` is followed immediately by square brackets enclosing one or more expressions separated by commas:[36]

> *symbol* '[' [*expression* [, *expression*] ...] ']'

It is important to note that the *symbol* that names the variable must be followed immediately by the "[", with **no** blank in between, or the construct will not be recognized as an indexed reference.

The *expressions* (separated by commas) between the brackets are called the *indexes* to the string. These index expressions are evaluated in turn from left to right, and each must evaluate to a value is of type `Rexx` or that can be converted to type `Rexx`.

The resulting index strings are taken "as-is" – that is, they must match exactly in content, case, and length for a reference to find a previously-set item. They may have any length (including the null string) and value (they are not constrained to be just those strings which are numbers, for example).

If a reference does not find a sub-value, then the non-indexed value of the variable is used.

Example:

```
surname='Unknown'              -- default value
surname['Fred']='Bloggs'
surname['Davy']='Jones'
try='Fred'
say surname[try] surname['Bert']
```

would say "`Bloggs Unknown`".

When multiple indexes are used, they indicate accessing a hierarchy of strings. A single NetRexx string has a single set of indexes and subvalues associated with it. The sub-values, however, are also NetRexx strings, and so may in turn have indexes and sub-values. When more than one index is specified in an indexed reference, the indexes are applied in turn from left to right to each retrieved sub-value.

---

36 The notations '[' and ']' indicate square brackets appearing in the NetRexx program.

For example, in the sequence:

```
x='?'
x['foo', 'bar']='OK'
say x['foo', 'bar']
y=x['foo']
say y['bar']
```

both **say** instructions would display the string "OK".

Indexed strings may be used to set up "associative arrays", or dictionaries, in which the subscript is not necessarily numeric, and thus offer great scope for the creative programmer. A useful application is to set up a variable in which the subscripts are taken from the value of one or more variables, so effecting a form of associative (content addressable) memory. The *justone* program (see page 19) is an example of this technique.

Notes:

1. A variable of type `Rexx` must have been assigned a value before indexing is used on it. This is the value that is used as the default value whenever an indexed reference finds no sub-value.
2. The indexes, and hence the sub-values, of a `Rexx` object can be retrieved in turn using the **over** (see page 89) keyword of the **loop** instruction.
3. The `exists` method (see page 156) of the `Rexx` class may be used to test whether an indexed reference has an explicitly-set value.
4. Assigning `null` to an indexed reference (for example, the assignment `switch[7]=null;`) drops the sub-value; until set to a new value, any reference to the sub-value (including use of the `exists` method) will return the same result as when it had never been set.

Arrays

In addition to indexed strings, NetRexx also includes the concept of fixed-size *arrays*, which may be used for indexing values of any type (including strings).

Arrays are used with the same syntax and in the same manner as indexed strings, but with important differences that allow for compact implementations and access to equivalent data structures constructed using other programming languages:

1. The indexes for arrays must be whole numbers that are zero or positive. There will usually be an implementation restriction on the maximum value of the index (typically 999999999 or higher).
2. The elements of an array are considered to be *ordered*; the first element has index `0`, the second `1`, and so on.
3. An array is of fixed size; it must be constructed before use.

4. Variables that are assigned arrays can only be assigned arrays (of the same dimension, see below) in the future. That is, being an array changes the type of a value; it becomes a *dimensioned type* (see page 40).

Array references use the NetRexx *indexed reference* syntax defined above. The same syntax is used for constructing arrays, except that the symbol before the left bracket describes a type (and hence may be qualified by a package name). The expression or expressions between the brackets indicate the size of the array in each dimension, and must be a positive whole number or zero:

```
arg=String[4]         -- makes an array for four Strings
arg=java.io.File[4]   -- makes an array for four Files
i=int[3]              -- makes an array for three 'int's
```

(Another way of describing this is that array constructors look just like other object constructors, except that brackets are used instead of parentheses.)

Once an array has been constructed, its elements can be referred to using brackets and expressions, as before:

```
i[2]=3 -- sets the '2'-indexed value of 'i'
j=i[2] -- sets 'j' to the '2'-indexed value of 'i'
```

Regular multiple-dimensioned arrays may be constructed and referenced by using multiple expressions within the brackets:

```
i=int[2,3] -- makes a 2x3 array of 'int' type objects
i[2,2]=3   -- sets the '2,2'-indexed value of 'i'
j=i[2,2]   -- sets 'j' to the '2,2'-indexed value of 'i'
```

As with indexed strings, when multiple indexes are used, they indicate accessing a hierarchy of arrays (the underlying model is therefore of a hierarchy of single-dimensioned arrays). When more than one index is specified in an indexed reference to an array, the indexes are applied in turn from left to right to each array.

As described in the section on *Types* (see page 39), the type of a variable that refers to an array can be set (declared) by assignment of the type with array notation that indicates the dimension of an array without any sizes:

```
k=int[]      -- one-dimensional array of 'int' objects
m=float[,,] -- 3-dimensional array of 'float' objects
```

The same syntax is also used when describing an array type in the arguments of a **method** instruction or when converting types. For example, after:

```
gg=char[] "Horse"
```

the variable `gg` has as its value an array of type `char[]` containing the five characters `H`, `o`, `r`, `s`, and `e`.

SECTION 12: KEYWORD INSTRUCTIONS

A *keyword instruction* is one or more clauses, the first of which starts with a keyword that identifies the instruction. Some keyword instructions affect the flow of control; the remainder just provide services to the programmer. Some keyword instructions (**do**, **if**, **loop**, or **select**) can include nested instructions.

As can be deduced from the syntax rules described earlier, a keyword instruction is recognized **only** if its keyword is the first token in a clause, and if the second token is not an "=" character (implying an assignment). It would also not be recognized if the second token started with "(", "[", or "." (implying that the first token starts a term).

Further, if a current local variable, method argument, or property has the same name as a keyword then the keyword will not be recognized. This important rule allows NetRexx to be extended with new keywords in the future without invalidating existing programs.

Thus, for example, this sequence in a program with no say variable:

```
say 'Hello'
say('1')
say=3
say 'Hello'
```

would be a **say** instruction, a call to some say method, an assignment to a say variable, and an error.

In NetRexx, therefore, keywords are not reserved; they may be used as the names of variables (though this is not recommended, where known in advance).

Certain other keywords, known as *sub–keywords*, may be known within the clauses of individual instructions – for example, the symbols **to** and **while** in the **loop** instruction. Again, these are not reserved; if they had been used as names of variables, they would not be recognized as sub-keywords.

Blanks adjacent to keywords have no effect other than that of separating the keyword from the subsequent token. For example, this applies to the blanks next to the sub-keyword **while** in

```
loop  while  a=3
```

Here at least one blank was required to separate the symbols forming the keywords and the variable name, a. However the blank following the **while** is not necessary in

```
loop while 'Me'=a
```

though it does aid readability.

SECTION 13: CLASS INSTRUCTION

class *name* [*visibility*] [*modifier*] [**binary**]
[**extends** *classname*]
[**uses** *useslist*]
[**implements** *interfacelist*] ;

where *visibility* is one of:

private
public

and *modifier* is one of:

abstract
final
interface

and *useslist* and *interfacelist* are lists of one or more *classnames*, separated by commas.

The **class** instruction is used to introduce a class, as described in the sections *Types and Classes* (see page 39) and *Program structure* (see page 115), and define its attributes. The class must be given a *name*, which must be different from the name of any other classes in the program. The *name*, which must be a non-numeric symbol, is known as the *short name* of the class.

A *classname* can be either the short name of a class (if that is unambiguous in the context in which it is used), or the qualified name of the class – the name of the class prefixed by a package name and a period, as described under the **package** instruction (see page 103).

The *body* of the class consists of all clauses following the class instruction (if any) until the next **class** instruction or the end of the program.

The *visibility*, *modifier*, and **binary** keywords, and the **extends**, **uses**, and **implements** phrases, may appear in any order.

Visibility

Classes may be **public** or **private**:

- A *public class* is visible to (that is, may be used by) all other classes.
- A *private class* is visible only within same program and to classes in the same package (see page 103).

A program may have only one public class, and if no class is marked public then the first is assumed to be public (unless it is explicitly marked private).

Modifier

Most classes are collections of data (properties) and the procedures that can act on that data (methods); they completely implement a datatype (type), and are permitted to be subclassed. These are called *standard classes*. The *modifier* keywords indicate that the class is not a standard class – it is special in some way. Only one of the following modifier keywords is allowed:

abstract

An *abstract class* does not completely implement a datatype; one or more of the methods that it defines (or which it inherits from classes it extends or implements) is abstract – that is, the name of the method and the types of its arguments are defined, but no instructions to implement the method are provided.

Since some methods are not provided, an object cannot be constructed from an abstract class. Instead, the class must be extended and any missing methods provided. Such a subclass can then be used to construct an object.

Abstract classes are useful where many subclasses can share common data or methods, but each will have some unique attribute or attributes (data and/or methods). For example, some set of geometric objects might share dimensions in X and Y, yet need unique methods for calculating the area of the object.

final

A *final class* is considered to be complete; it cannot be subclassed (extended), and all its methods are considered complete.[37]

interface

An *interface class* is an abstract class that contains only abstract method definitions and/or constants. That is, it defines neither instructions that implement methods nor modifiable properties, and hence cannot be used to construct an object.

Interface classes are used by classes that claim to *implement* them (see the **implements** keyword, described below). The primary difference between abstract and interface classes is that the former may have methods which are not abstract, and hence can only be subclassed (extended), whereas the latter are wholly abstract and so may be both extended (to make a new interface class) and/or implemented.

Interface classes may not be **private**; any properties in an interface class are both **public** and **constant**.

---

37 This modifier is provided for consistency with other languages, and may allow compilers to improve the performance of classes that refer to the final class. In many cases it will reduce the reusability of the class, and hence should be avoided.

Binary

The keyword **binary** indicates that the class is a *binary class.* In binary classes, literal strings and numeric symbols are assigned native string or binary (primitive) types, rather than NetRexx types, and native binary operations are used to implement operators where possible. When **binary** is not in effect (the default), terms in expressions are converted to NetRexx types before use by operators. The section *Binary values and operations* (see page 142) describes the implications of binary classes in detail.

Extends

Classes form a hierarchy, with all classes (except the top of the tree, the `Object`[38] class) being a *subclass* of some other class. The **extends** keyword identifies the *classname* of the immediate *superclass* of the new class – that is, the class immediately above it in the hierarchy. If no **extends** phrase is given, the superclass is assumed to be `Object` (or `null`, in the case where the current class is `Object`).

Uses

The **uses** keyword introduces a list of the names of one or more classes that will be used as a source of constant (or static) properties and/or methods.

When a term (see page 41) starts with a symbol, method call, or indexed reference that is not known in the current context, each class in the *useslist* and its superclasses are searched (in the order specified in the *useslist*) for a constant or static method or property that matches the item. If found, the method or property is used just as though explicitly qualified by the name of the class in which it was found.

The **uses** mechanism affects only the syntax of terms in the current class; it is not inherited by subclasses of the current class.

Implements

The **implements** keyword introduces a list of the names of one or more interface classes (see above). These interface classes are then known to (inherited by) the current class, in the order specified in the *interfacelist*. Their methods (which are all abstract) and constant properties act as though part of the current class, unless they are overridden (hidden) by a method or constant of the same name in the current class.

If the current class is not an interface class then it must implement (provide non-abstract methods for) all the methods inherited from the interface classes in the implements list.

Interface classes, therefore, can be used to:

---

[38] *In the reference implementation,* `java.lang.Object`.

1. Define a common set of methods (possibly with associated constants) that will be implemented by other classes.
2. Conveniently package collections of constants for use by other classes.

The implements list may not include the superclass of the current class.

SECTION 14: DO INSTRUCTION

> **do** [**label** *name*] [**protect** *term*] ;
> *instructionlist*
> [**catch** [*vare* =] *exception* ; *instructionlist*] ...
> [**finally** [;] *instructionlist*]
> **end** [*name*] ;
>
> where *name* is a non-numeric *symbol*
>
> and *instructionlist* is zero or more *instructions*.

The **do** instruction is used to group instructions together for execution; these are executed once. The group may optionally be given a label, and may protect an object while the instructions in the group are executed; exceptional conditions can be handled with **catch** and **finally**.

The most common use of **do** is simply for treating a number of instructions as group.

Example:

```
/* The two instructions between DO and END will both */
/* be executed if A has the value 3.                 */
if a=3 then do
  a=a+2
  say 'Smile!'
  end
```

Here, only the first *instructionlist* is used. This forms the *body* of the group.

The instructions in the *instructionlists* may be any assignment, method call, or keyword instruction, including any of the more complex constructions such as **loop**, **if**, **select**, and the **do** instruction itself.

Label phrase

If **label** is used to specify a *name* for the group, then a **leave** which specifies that name may be used to leave the group, and the **end** that ends the group may optionally specify the name of the group for additional checking.

Example:

```
do label sticky
  x=ask
  if x='quit' then leave sticky
  say 'x was' x
  end sticky
```

Protect phrase

If **protect** is given it must be followed by a *term* that evaluates to a value that is not just a type and is not of a primitive type; while the **do** construct is being executed, the value (object) is protected – that is, all the instructions in the **do** construct have exclusive access to the object.

Both **label** and **protect** may be specified, in any order, if required.

Exceptions in do groups

Exceptions that are raised by the instructions within a do group may be caught using one or more **catch** clauses that name the *exception* that they will catch. When an exception is caught, the exception object that holds the details of the exception may optionally be assigned to a variable, *vare*.

Similarly, a **finally** clause may be used to introduce instructions that will always be executed at the end of the group, even if an exception is raised (whether caught or not).

The *Exceptions* section (see page 145) has details and examples of **catch** and **finally**.

SECTION 15: EXIT INSTRUCTION

exit [*expression*] ;

exit is used to unconditionally leave a program, and optionally return a result to the caller. The entire program is terminated immediately.

If an *expression* is given, it is evaluated and the result of the evaluation is then passed back to the caller in an implementation-dependent manner when the program terminates. Typically this value is expected to be a small whole number; most implementations will accept values in the range 0 through 250. If no expression is given, a default result (which depends on the implementation, and is typically zero) is passed back to the caller.

Example:

```
j=3
exit j*4
/* Would exit with the value '12' */
```

"Running off the end" of a program is equivalent to the instruction `return;`. In the case where the program is simply a stand-alone application with no **class** or **method** instructions, this has the same effect as `exit;`, in that it terminates the whole program and returns a default result.

SECTION 16: IF INSTRUCTION

if *expression* [;]
  then [;] *instruction*
 [**else** [;] *instruction*]

The **if** construct is used to conditionally execute an instruction or group of instructions. It can also be used to select between two alternatives.

The expression is evaluated and must result in either 0 or 1. If the result was 1 (true) then the instruction after the **then** is executed. If the result was 0 (false) and an **else** was given then the instruction after the **else** is executed.

Example:

```
if answer='Yes' then say 'OK!'
                else say 'Why not?'
```

Remember that if the **else** clause is on the same line as the last clause of the **then** part, then you need a semicolon to terminate that clause.

Example:

```
if answer='Yes' then say 'OK!';  else say 'Why not?'
```

The **else** binds to the nearest **then** at the same level. This means that any **if** that is used as the instruction following the **then** in an **if** construct that has an **else** clause, must itself have an **else** clause (which may be followed by the dummy instruction, **nop**).

Example:

```
if answer='Yes' then if name='Fred' then say 'OK, Fred.'
                                    else say 'OK.'
                else say 'Why not?'
```

To include more than one instruction following **then** or **else**, use a grouping instruction (**do**, **loop**, or **select**).

Example:

```
if answer='Yes' then do
  say 'Line one of two'
  say 'Line two of two'
  end
```

In this instance, both **say** instructions are executed when the result of the **if** expression is 1.

Notes:

1. An *instruction* may be any assignment, method call, or keyword instruction, including any of the more complex constructions such as **do**, **loop**, **select**, and the **if** instruction itself. A null clause is not an instruction, however, so putting an extra semicolon after the **then** or **else** is not equivalent to putting a dummy instruction (as it would be in C or PL/I). The **nop** instruction is provided for this purpose.

2. The keyword **then** is treated specially, in that it need not start a clause. This allows the expression on the **if** clause to be terminated by the **then**, without a ";" being required – were this not so, people used to other computer languages would be inconvenienced. Hence the symbol **then** cannot be used as a variable name within the expression.[39]

SECTION 17: IMPORT INSTRUCTION

> **import** *name* ;
>
> where *name* is one or more non-numeric *symbol*s separated by periods, with an optional trailing period.

The **import** instruction is used to simplify the use of classes from other packages. If a class is identified by an **import** instruction, it can then be referred to by its short name, as given on the **class** instruction (see page 74), as well as by its fully qualified name.

There may be zero or more **import** instructions in a program. They must precede any **class** instruction (or any instruction that would start the default class).

In the following description, a *package name* names a package as described under the **package** instruction (see page 103).

The import *name* must be one of:

- A qualified class name, which is a package name immediately followed by a period which is immediately followed by a short class name – in this case, the individual class identified is imported.
- A package name – in this case, all the classes in the specified package are imported.
- A partial package name (a package name with one or more parts omitted from the right, indicated by a trailing period after the parts that are

---

39 Strictly speaking, **then** should only be recognized if not the name of a variable. In this special case, however, NetRexx language processors are permitted to treat **then** as reserved in the context of an **if** clause, to provide better performance and more useful error reporting.

present) – in this case, all classes in the package hierarchy below the specified point are imported.

Examples:

```
import java.lang.String
import java.lang
import java.
```

The first example above imports a single class (which could then be referred to simply as "`String`"). The second example imports all classes in the "`java.lang`" package. The third example imports all classes in all the packages whose name starts with "`java.`".

If two (or more) classes with the same short name are imported, then an attempt to use that short name as a class name or type is an error, as the reference would be ambiguous.

In the reference implementation, all classes in the "`java.`" and "`netrexx.`" hierarchies are imported by default, as though the two instructions:

```
import netrexx.
import java.
```

had been executed before the program begins.

SECTION 18: ITERATE INSTRUCTION

> **iterate** [*name*] ;
>
> where *name* is a non-numeric *symbol.*

iterate alters the flow of control within a **loop** construct. It may only be used in the body (the first *instructionlist*) of the construct.

Execution of the instruction list stops, and control is passed directly back up to the **loop** clause just as though the last clause in the body of the construct had just been executed. The control variable (if any) is then stepped (iterated) and termination conditions tested as normal and the instruction list is executed again, unless the loop is terminated by the **loop** clause.

If no *name* is specified, then **iterate** will step the innermost active loop.

If a *name* is specified, then it must be the name of the label, or control variable if there is no label, of a currently active loop (which may be the innermost), and this is the loop that is iterated. Any active **do**, **loop**, or **select** constructs inside the loop selected for iteration are terminated (as though by a **leave** instruction).

Example:

```
loop i=1 to 4
  if i=2 then iterate i
  say i
  end
/* Would display the numbers:  1, 3, 4  */
```

Notes:

1. A loop is active if it is currently being executed. If a method (even in the same class) is called during execution of a loop, then the loop becomes inactive until the method has returned. **iterate** cannot be used to step an inactive loop.

2. The *name* symbol, if specified, must exactly match the label (or the name of the control variable, if there is no label) in the **loop** clause in all respects except case.

SECTION 19: LEAVE INSTRUCTION

> **leave** [*name*];
>
> where *name* is a non-numeric *symbol*.

leave causes immediate exit from one or more **do**, **loop**, or **select** constructs. It may only be used in the body (the first *instructionlist*) of the construct.

Execution of the instruction list is terminated, and control is passed to the **end** clause of the construct, just as though the last clause in the body of the construct had just been executed or (if a loop) the termination condition had been met normally, except that on exit the control variable (if any) will contain the value it had when the **leave** instruction was executed.

If no *name* is specified, then **leave** must be within an active loop and will terminate the innermost active loop.

If a *name* is specified, then it must be the name of the label (or control variable for a loop with no label), of a currently active **do**, **loop**, or **select** construct (which may be the innermost). That construct (and any active constructs inside it) is then terminated. Control then passes to the clause following the **end** clause that matches the **do**, **loop**, or **select** clause identified by the *name*.

Example:

```
loop i=1 to 5
  say i
  if i=3 then leave
  end i
/* Would display the numbers:  1, 2, 3  */
```

Notes:

1. If any construct being left includes a **finally** clause, the *instructionlist* following the **finally** will be executed before the construct is left.
2. A **do**, **loop**, or **select** construct is active if it is currently being executed. If a method (even in the same class) is called during execution of an active construct, then the construct becomes inactive until the method has returned. **leave** cannot be used to leave an inactive construct.
3. The *name* symbol, if specified, must exactly match the label (or the name of the control variable, for a loop with no label) in the **do**, **loop**, or **select** clause in all respects except case.

SECTION 20: LOOP INSTRUCTION

loop [**label** *name*] [**protect** *termp*] [*repetitor*] [*conditional*] ;
instructionlist
[**catch** [*vare* =] *exception* ; *instructionlist*] ...
[**finally** [;] *instructionlist*]
end [*name*] ;

where *repetitor* is one of:

varc = *expri* [**to** *exprt*] [**by** *exprb*] [**for** *exprf*]
varo **over** *termo*
for *exprr*
forever

and *conditional* is either of:

while *exprw*
until *expru*

and *name* is a non-numeric *symbol*

and *instructionlist* is zero or more *instructions*

and *expri*, *exprt*, *exprb*, *exprf*, *exprr*, *exprw*, and *expru* are *expressions*.

The **loop** instruction is used to group instructions together and execute them repetitively. The loop may optionally be given a label, and may protect an object while the instructions in the loop are executed; exceptional conditions can be handled with **catch** and **finally**.

loop is the most complicated of the NetRexx keyword instructions. It can be used as a simple indefinite loop, a predetermined repetitive loop, as a loop with a bounding condition that is recalculated on each iteration, or as a loop that steps over the contents of a collection of values.

Syntax notes:

- The **label** and **protect** phrases may be in any order. They must precede any *repetitor* or *conditional*.
- The first *instructionlist* is known as the *body* of the loop.
- The **to**, **by**, and **for** phrases in the first form of *repetitor* may be in any order, if used, and will be evaluated in the order they are written.
- Any instruction allowed in a method is allowed in an *instructionlist*, including assignments, method call instructions, and keyword

instructions (including any of the more complex constructions such as **if**, **do**, **select**, or the **loop** instruction itself).

- If **for** or **forever** start the *repetitor* and are followed by an "=" character, they are taken as control variable names, not keywords (as for assignment instructions).
- The expressions *expri*, *exprt*, *exprb*, or *exprf* will be ended by any of the keywords **to**, **by**, **for**, **while**, or **until** (unless the word is the name of a variable).
- The expressions *exprw* or *expru* will be ended by either of the keywords **while** or **until** (unless the word is the name of a variable).

Indefinite loops

If neither *repetitor* nor *conditional* are present, or the *repetitor* is the keyword **forever**, then the loop is an *indefinite loop*. It will be ended only when some instruction in the first *instructionlist* causes control to leave the loop.

Example:

```
/* This displays "Go caving!" at least once */
loop forever
  say 'Go caving!'
  if ask='' then leave
  end
```

Bounded loops

If a *repetitor* (other than **forever**) or *conditional* is given, the first *instructionlist* forms a *bounded loop*, and the instruction list is executed according to any *repetitor phrase*, optionally modified by a *conditional phrase*.

Simple bounded loops

When the *repetitor* starts with the keyword **for**, the expression *exprr* is evaluated immediately (with 0 added, to effect any rounding) to give a repetition count, which must be a whole number that is zero or positive. The loop is then executed that many times, unless it is terminated by some other condition.

Example:

```
/* This displays "Hello" five times */
loop for 5
  say 'Hello'
  end
```

Controlled bounded loops

A *controlled loop* begins with an *assignment*, which can be identified by the "=" that follows the name of a control variable, *varc*. The control variable is assigned an initial value (the result of *expri*, formatted as though 0 had been added) before the first execution of the instruction list. The control variable is then stepped (by adding the result of *exprb*) before the second and subsequent times that the instruction list is executed.

The name of the control variable, *varc*, must be a non-numeric symbol that names an existing a new variable in the current method or a property in the current class (that is, it cannot be element of an array, the property of a superclass, or a more complex term). It is further restricted in that it must not already be used as the name of a control variable or label in a loop (or **do** or **select** construct) that encloses the new loop.

The instruction list in the body of the loop is executed repeatedly while the end condition (determined by the result of *exprt*) is not met. If *exprb* is positive or zero, then the loop will be terminated when *varc* is greater than the result of *exprt*. If negative, then the loop will be terminated when *varc* is less than the result of *exprt*.

The expressions *exprt* and *exprb* must result in numbers. They are evaluated once only (with 0 added, to effect any rounding), in the order they appear in the instruction, and before the loop begins and before *expri* (which must also result in a number) is evaluated and the control variable is set to its initial value.

The default value for *exprb* is 1. If no *exprt* is given then the loop will execute indefinitely unless it is terminated by some other condition.

Example:

```
loop i=3 to -2 by -1
  say i
  end
/* Would display: 3, 2, 1, 0, -1, -2 */
```

Note that the numbers do not have to be whole numbers:

Example:

```
x=0.3
loop y=x to x+4 by 0.7
  say y
  end
/* Would display: 0.3, 1.0, 1.7, 2.4, 3.1, 3.8 */
```

The control variable may be altered within the loop, and this may affect the iteration of the loop. Altering the value of the control variable in this way is normally considered to be suspect programming practice, though it may be appropriate in certain circumstances.

Note that the end condition is tested at the start of each iteration (and after the control variable is stepped, on the second and subsequent iterations). It is therefore possible for the body of the loop to be skipped entirely if the end condition is met immediately.

The execution of a controlled loop may further be bounded by a **for** phrase. In this case, *exprf* must be given and must evaluate to a non-negative whole number. This acts just like the repetition count in a simple bounded loop, and sets a limit to the number of iterations around the loop if it is not terminated by some other condition.

exprf is evaluated along with the expressions *exprt* and *exprb*. That is, it is evaluated once only (with `0` added), when the **loop** instruction is first executed and before the control variable is given its initial value; the three expressions are evaluated in the order in which they appear. Like the **to** condition, the **for** count is checked at the start of each iteration, as shown in the programmer's model (see page 92).

Example:

```
loop y=0.3 to 4.3 by 0.7 for 3
  say y
  end
/* Would display: 0.3, 1.0, 1.7 */
```

In a controlled loop, the symbol that describes the control variable may be specified on the **end** clause (unless a label is specified, see below). NetRexx will then check that this symbol exactly matches the *varc* of the control variable in the **loop** clause (in all respects except case). If the symbol does not match, then the program is in error – this enables the nesting of loops to be checked automatically.

Example:

```
loop k=1 to 10
  ...
  ...
  end k  /* Checks this is the END for K loop */
```

Note: The values taken by the control variable may be affected by the **numeric** settings, since normal NetRexx arithmetic rules apply to the computation of stepping the control variable.

Over loops

When the second token of the *repetitor* is the keyword **over**, the control variable, *varo* is used to work through the sub-values in the collection of indexed strings identified by *termo*. In this case, the **loop** instruction takes a "snapshot" of the indexes in the collection at the start of the loop, and then for each iteration of the loop the control variable is set to the next available index from the snapshot.

The number of iterations of the loop will be the number of indexes in the collection, unless the loop is terminated by some other condition.

Example:

```
mycoll=''
mycoll['Tom']=1
mycoll['Dick']=2
mycoll['Harry']=3
loop name over mycoll
  say mycoll[name]
  end
/* might display: 3, 1, 2 */
```

Notes:

1. The order in which the values are returned are undefined; all that is known is that all indexes available when the loop started will be recorded and assigned to *varo* in turn as the loop iterates.
2. The same restrictions apply to *varo* as apply to *varc*, the control variable for controlled loops (see above).
3. Similarly, the symbol *varo* may be used as a name for the loop and be specified on the **end** clause (unless a label is specified, see below).

In the reference implementation, the **over** *form of repetitor may also be used to step though the contents of any object that is of a type that is a subclass of* `java.util.Dictionary`*, such as an object of type* `java.util.Hashtable`*. In this case, termo specifies the dictionary, and a snapshot (enumeration) of the keys to the Dictionary is taken at the start of the loop. Each iteration of the loop then assigns a new key to the control variable varo which must be (or will be given, if it is new) the type* `java.lang.Object`.

Conditional phrases

Any of the forms of loop syntax can be followed by a *conditional* phrase which may cause termination of the loop.

If **while** is specified, *exprw* is evaluated, using the latest values of all variables in the expression, before the instruction list is executed on every iteration, and after the control variable (if any) is stepped. The expression must evaluate to either 0 or 1, and the instruction list will be repeatedly executed while the result is 1 (that is, the loop ends if the expression evaluates to 0).

Example:

```
loop i=1 to 10 by 2 while i<6
  say i
  end
/* Would display: 1, 3, 5 */
```

If **until** is specified, *expru* is evaluated, using the latest values of all variables in the expression, on the second and subsequent iterations, and before the control variable (if any) is stepped.[40] The expression must evaluate to either 0 or 1, and the instruction list will be repeatedly executed until the result is 1 (that is, the loop ends if the expression evaluates to 1).

Example:

```
loop i=1 to 10 by 2 until i>6
  say i
  end
/* Would display: 1, 3, 5, 7 */
```

Note that the execution of loops may also be modified by using the **iterate** or **leave** instructions.

Label phrase

The **label** phrase may used to specify a *name* for the loop. The name can then optionally be used on

- a **leave** instruction, to specify the name of the loop to leave
- an **iterate** instruction, to specify the name of the loop to be iterated
- the **end** clause of the loop, to confirm the identity of the loop that is being ended, for additional checking.

---

40 Thus, it appears that the **until** condition is tested after the instruction list is executed on each iteration. However, it is the **loop** clause that carries out the evaluation.

Example:

```
loop label pooks i=1 to 10
  loop label hill while j<3
    ...
    if a=b then leave pooks
    ...
    end hill
  end pooks
```

In this example, the **leave** instruction leaves both loops.

If a label is specified using the **label** keyword, it overrides any name derived from the control variable name (if any). That is, the variable name cannot be used to refer to the loop if a label is specified.

Protect phrase

The **protect** phrase may used to specify a term, *termp*, that evaluates to a value that is not just a type and is not of a primitive type; while the **loop** construct is being executed, the value (object) is protected – that is, all the instructions in the **loop** construct have exclusive access to the object.

Example:

```
loop protect myobject while a<b
  ...
  end
```

Both **label** and **protect** may be specified, in any order, if required.

Exceptions in loops

Exceptions that are raised by the instructions within a **loop** construct may be caught using one or more **catch** clauses that name the *exception* that they will catch. When an exception is caught, the exception object that holds the details of the exception may optionally be assigned to a variable, *vare*.

Similarly, a **finally** clause may be used to introduce instructions that will always be executed when the loop ends, even if an exception is raised (whether caught or not).

The *Exceptions* section (see page 145) has details and examples of **catch** and **finally**.

Programmer's model – how a typical loop is executed

This model forms part of the definition of the **loop** instruction.

For the following loop:

loop *varc* = *expri* **to** *exprt* **by** *exprb* **while** *exprw*

...

instruction list

...

end

NetRexx will execute the following:

```
    $tempt=exprt+0    /* ($variables are internal and    */
    $tempb=exprb+0    /*   are not accessible.)          */
    varc=expri+0
    Transfer control to the point identified as $start:

$loop:
    /* An UNTIL expression would be tested here, with: */
    /* if expru then leave                              */
    varc=varc + $tempb
$start:
    if varc > $tempt then leave    /* leave quits a loop */
    /* A FOR count would be checked here                */
    if \exprw then leave
       ...
       instruction list
       ...
    Transfer control to the point identified as $loop:
```

Notes:

1. This example is for *exprb* `>= 0`. For a negative *exprb*, the test at the start point of the loop would use "<" rather than ">".
2. The upwards transfer of control takes place at the end of the body of the loop, immediately before the **end** clause (or any **catch** or **finally** clause). The **end** clause is only reached when the loop is finally completed.

SECTION 21: METHOD INSTRUCTION

method *name*[([*arglist*])]
[*visibility*] [*modifier*] [**protect**]
[**returns** *termr*]
[**signals** *signallist*] ;

where *arglist* is a list of one or more *assignments*, separated by commas

and *visibility* is one of:

inheritable
private
public

and *modifier* is one of:

abstract
constant
final
native
static

and *signallist* is a list of one or more *terms*, separated by commas.

The **method** instruction is used to introduce a method within a class, as described in *Program structure* (see page 115), and define its attributes. The method must be given a *name*, which must be a non-numeric symbol. This is its *short name.*

If the short name of a method matches the short name of the class in which it appears, it is a *constructor method.* Constructor methods are used for constructing values (objects), and are described in detail in *Methods and Constructors* (see page 47).

The *body* of the method consists of all clauses following the method instruction (if any) until the next **method** or **class** instruction, or the end of the program.

The *visibility*, *modifier*, and **protect** keywords, and the **returns** and **signals** phrases, may appear in any order.

Arguments

The *arglist* on a **method** instruction, immediately following the method name, is optional and defines a list of the arguments for the method. An *argument* is a value that was provided by the caller when the method was invoked.

If there are no arguments, this may be optionally be indicated by an "empty" pair of parentheses.

In the *arglist*, each argument has the syntax of an *assignment* (see page 65), where the "=" and the following *expression* may be omitted. The name in the assignment provides the name for the argument (which must not be the same as the name of any property in the class). Each argument is also optionally assigned a type, or type and default value, following the usual rules of assignment. If there is no assignment, the argument is assigned the NetRexx string type, `Rexx`.

If there is no assignment (that is, there is no "=") or the expression to the right of the "=" returns just a type, the argument is *required* (that is, it must always be specified by the caller when the method is invoked).

If an explicit value is given by the expression then the argument is *optional*; when the caller does not provide an argument in that position, then the expression is evaluated when the method is invoked and the result is provided to the method as the argument.

Optional arguments may be omitted "from the right" only. That is, arguments may not be omitted to the left of arguments that are not omitted.

Examples:

```
method fred
method fred()
method fred(width, height)
method fred(width=int, height=int 10)
```

In these examples, the first two **method** instructions are equivalent, and take no arguments. The third example takes two arguments, which are both strings of type `Rexx`. The final example takes two arguments, both of type `int`; the second argument is optional, and if not supplied will default to the value 10 (note that any valid expression could be used for the default value).

Visibility

Methods may be **public**, **inheritable**, or **private**:

- A *public method* is visible to (that is, may be used by) all other classes to which the current class is visible.
- An *inheritable method* is visible to (that is, may be used by) only those classes that extend (that is, are subclasses of) or implement the current class.
- A *private method* is visible only within the current class.

By default (*i.e.*, if no visibility keyword is specified), methods are public.

Modifier

Most methods consist of instructions that follow the **method** instruction and implement the method; the method is associated with an object constructed by the class. These are called *standard methods*. The *modifier* keywords define that the method is not a standard method – it is special in some way. Only one of the following modifier keywords is allowed:

abstract

An *abstract method* has the name of the method and the types (but not values) of its arguments defined, but no instructions to implement the method are provided (or permitted).

If a class contains any abstract methods, an object cannot be constructed from it, and so the class itself must be abstract; the **abstract** keyword must be present on the **class** instruction (see page 74).

Within an interface class, the **abstract** keyword is optional on the methods of the class, as all methods must be abstract. No other *modifier* is allowed on the methods of an interface class.

constant

A *constant method* is a static method that cannot be overridden by a method in a subclass of the current class. That is, it is both **final** and **static** (see below).

final

A *final method* is considered to be complete; it cannot be overridden by a subclass of the current class. **private** methods are implicitly **final**.[41]

native

A *native method* is a method that is implemented by the environment, not by instructions in the current class. Such methods have no NetRexx instructions to implement the method (and none are permitted), and they cannot be overridden by a method in a subclass of the current class.

Native methods are used for accessing primitive operations provided by the underlying operating system or by implementation-dependent packages.

static

A *static method* is a method that is not a constructor and is associated with the class, rather than with an object constructed by the class. It cannot use properties directly, except those that are also static (or constant).

---

41 This modifier may allow compilers to improve the performance of methods that are final, but may also reduce the reusability of the class.

Static methods may be invoked in the following ways:

1. Within the initialization expression of a static or constant property (such methods are invoked when the class is first loaded).
2. By qualifying the name of the method with the name of its class (qualified by the package name if necessary), for example, using "`Math.Sin(1.3)`" or "`java.lang.Math.Sin(1.3)`". Methods called in this way are in effect *functions*.
3. By implicitly qualifying the name by including the name of its class in the **uses** phrase in the **class** instruction for the current class. Static methods in classes listed in this way can be used directly, without qualification, for example, as "`Sin(1.3)`". They may be still be qualified, if preferred.

In the reference implementation, stand-alone applications are started by the `java` *command invoking a static method called* `main` *which takes a single argument (of type* `java.lang.String[]`*) and returns no result.*

Protect

The keyword **protect** indicates that the method protects the current object (or class, for a static method) while the instructions in the method are executed. That is, the instructions in the method have exclusive access to the object; if some other method (or construct) is executing in parallel with the invocation of the method and is protecting the same object then the method will not start execution until the object is no longer protected.

Note that if a method or construct protecting an object invokes a method (or starts a new construct) that protects the same object then execution continues normally. The inner method or construct is not prevented from executing, because it is not executing in parallel.

Returns

The **returns** keyword is followed by a term, *termr*, that must evaluate to a type. This type is used to define the type of values returned by **return** instructions within the method.

The **returns** phrase is only required if the method is to return values of a type that is not NetRexx strings (class `Rexx`). If **returns** is specified, all **return** instructions (see page 107) within the method must specify an expression.

Example:

```
method filer(path, name) returns File
  return File(path||name)
```

This method always returns a value which is a `File` object.

Signals

The **signals** keyword introduces a list of terms that evaluate to types that are Exceptions (see page 145). This list enumerates and documents the exceptions that are signalled within the method (or by a method which is called from the current method) but are not caught by a **catch** clause in a control construct.

Example:

```
method soup(cat) signals IOException, DivideByZero
```

It is considered good programming practice to use this list to document "unusual" exceptions signalled by a method. Implementations that support the concept of checked exceptions (see page 147) must report as an error any checked exception that is incorrectly included in the list (that is, if the exception is never signalled or would always be caught). Such implementations may also offer an option that enforces the listing of all or some checked exceptions.

Duplicate methods

Methods may not duplicate properties or other methods in the same class. Specifically:

- The short name of a method must not be the same as the name of any property in the same class.
- The number (zero or more) and types of the arguments of a method (or any subset permitted by omitting optional arguments) must not be the same as those of any other method of the same name in the class (also checking any subset permitted by omitting optional arguments).

Note that the second rule does allow multiple methods with the same name in a class, provided that the number of arguments differ or at least one argument differs in type.

SECTION 22: NOP INSTRUCTION

nop ;

nop is a dummy instruction that has no effect. It can be useful as an explicit "do nothing" instruction following a **then** or **else** clause.

Example:

```
select
  when a=b then nop             -- Do nothing
  when a>b then say 'A > B'
  otherwise     say 'A < B'
  end
```

Note: Putting an extra semicolon instead of the **nop** would merely insert a null clause, which would just be ignored by NetRexx. The second **when** clause would then immediately follow the **then**, and hence would be reported as an error. **nop** is a true instruction, however, and is therefore a valid target for the **then** clause.

SECTION 23: NUMERIC INSTRUCTION

numeric { **digits** [*exprd*] | **form** [**scientific** | **engineering**] } ;

where *exprd* is an *expression*.

The **numeric** instruction is used to change the way in which arithmetic operations are carried out by a program. The effects of this instruction are described in detail in the section on *Numbers and Arithmetic* (see page 130).

numeric digits

controls the precision under which arithmetic operations will be evaluated (see page 132). If no expression *exprd* is given then the default value of 9 is used. Otherwise the result of the expression is rounded, if necessary, according to the current setting of **numeric digits** before it is used. The value used must be a positive whole number.

There is normally no limit to the value for **numeric digits** (except the constraints imposed by the amount of storage and other resources available) but note that high precisions are likely to be expensive in processing time. It is recommended that the default value be used wherever possible.

Note that small values of **numeric digits** (for example, values less than 6) are generally only useful for very specialized applications. The setting of **numeric digits** affects all computations, so even the operation of loops may be affected by rounding if small values are used.

If an implementation does not support a requested value for **numeric digits** then the instruction will fail with an exception (which may, as usual, be caught with the **catch** clause of a control construct).

The current setting of **numeric digits** may be retrieved with the `digits` special word (see page 118).

numeric form

controls which form of exponential notation (see page 139) is to be used for the results of operations. This may be either *scientific* (in which case only one, non-zero, digit will appear before the decimal point), or *engineering* (in which case the power of ten will always be a multiple of three, and the part before the decimal point will be in the range 1 through 999). The default notation is scientific.

The form is set directly by the sub-keywords **scientific** or **engineering**; if neither sub-keyword is given, **scientific** is assumed. The current setting of **numeric form** may be retrieved with the `form` special word (see page 118).

If an implementation does not support a requested value for **numeric form** then the instruction will fail with an exception (which may, as usual, be caught with the **catch** clause of a control construct).

The **numeric** instruction may be used where needed as a dynamically executed instruction in a method.

It may also appear, more than once if necessary, before the first method in a class, in which case it forms the default setting for the initialization of subsequent properties in the class and for all methods in the class. In this case, any exception due to the **numeric** instruction is raised when the class is first loaded.

SECTION 24: OPTIONS INSTRUCTION

> **options** *wordlist* ;
>
> where *wordlist* is one or more *symbols* separated by blanks.

The **options** instruction is used to pass special requests to the language processor (for example, an interpreter or compiler).

Individual words, known as *option words*, in the *wordlist* which are meaningful to the language processor will be obeyed (these might control optimizations, enforce standards, enable implementation-dependent features, *etc.*); those which are not recognized will be ignored (they are assumed to be instructions to a different language processor). Option words in the list that are known will be recognized independently of case.

There may be zero or more **options** instructions in a program. They apply to the whole program, and must come before the first **class** instruction (or any instruction that starts a class).

In the reference implementation, the known option words are:

binary

All classes in this program will be binary classes (see page 76). In binary classes, literals are assigned binary (primitive) or native string types, rather than NetRexx types, and native binary operations are used to implement operators where appropriate, as described in "Binary values and operations" (see page 142) . In classes that are not binary, terms in expressions are converted to the NetRexx string type, `Rexx`*, before use by operators.*

crossref

Requests that cross-reference listings of variables be displayed, by class.

diag

Requests that diagnostic information (for experimental use only) be displayed. The **diag** *option word may also have side-effects.*

format

Requests that the translator output file (Java source code) be formatted for improved readability. Note that if this option is in effect, line numbers from the input file will not be preserved (so run-time errors and exception trace-backs may show incorrect line numbers).

logo

Requests that the language processor display an introductory logotype sequence (name and version of the compiler or interpreter, etc.).

replace

Requests that replacement of the translator output (`.java`*) file be allowed. The default,* **noreplace**, *prevents an existing* `.java` *file being accidentally overwritten.*

strictargs

Requires that method invocations always specify parentheses, even when no arguments are supplied.

strictassign

Requires that only exact type matches be allowed in assignments (this is stronger than Java requirements). This also applies to the matching of arguments in method calls.

strictcase

Requires that local and external name comparisons for variables, properties, methods, classes, and special words match in case (that is, names must be identical to match).

strictsignal

Requires that all checked exceptions (see page 147) signalled within a method but not caught by a **catch** *clause be listed in the* **signals** *phrase of the method instruction.*

trace

If given, **trace** *instructions are accepted. If* **notrace** *is given, then trace instructions are ignored. The latter can be useful to prevent tracing overheads while leaving* **trace** *instructions in a program.*

utf8

If given, clauses following the **options** *instruction are expected to be encoded using UTF-8, so all Unicode characters may be used in the source of the program.*

In UTF-8 encoding, Unicode characters less than `'\u0080'` *are represented using one byte (whose most-significant bit is 0), characters in the range* `'\u0080'` *through* `'\u07FF'` *are encoded as two bytes, in the sequence of bits:*

```
110xxxxx 10xxxxxx
```

where the eleven digits shown as `x` *are the least significant eleven bits of the character, and characters in the range* `'\u0800'` *through* `'\uFFFF'` *are encoded as three bytes, in the sequence of bits:*

```
1110xxxx 10xxxxxx 10xxxxxx
```

where the sixteen digits shown as `x` *are the sixteen bits of the character.*

If **noutf8** *is given, following clauses are assumed to comprise only Unicode characters in the range* `'\x00'` *through* `'\xFF'`*, with the more significant byte of the encoding of each character being 0.*

verbose, verboseX

Sets the "noisiness" of the language processor. The digit X may be any of the digits `0` *through* `5`*; if omitted, a value of* `3` *is used. The options* **noverbose** *and* **verbose0** *both suppress all messages except errors and warnings.*

*Prefixing any of the above with "**no**" turns the selected option off.*

Example:

```
options binary nocrossref nostrictassign strictargs
```

The default settings of the various options are:

```
nobinary crossref nodiag noformat logo noreplace
nostrictargs nostrictassign nostrictcase nostrictsignal
trace noutf8 verbose3
```

When an option word is repeated (in the same **options** *instruction or not), or conflicting option words are specified, then the last use determines the state of the option.*

All option words may also be set as command line options when invoking the processor, by prefixing them with "-":

Example:

```
java netrexx.process.NetRexxC -format -verbose4 foo.nrx
```

In this case, the options may come before or after file specifications.

Options set with the **options** *instruction override command-line settings, following the "last use" rule.*

For more information, see the installation and user documentation for your implementation.

SECTION 25: PACKAGE INSTRUCTION

> **package** *name* ;
>
> where *name* is one or more non-numeric *symbol*s separated by periods.

The **package** instruction is used to define the package to which the class or classes in the current program belong.

Classes that belong to the same package have privileged access to other classes in the same package, in that each class is visible to all other classes in the same package, even if not declared public. Packages also conveniently group classes for use by the **import** instruction (see page 81).

The *name* must specify a *package name*, which is one or more non-numeric symbols, separated by periods, with no blanks.

There must be at most one **package** instruction in a program. It must precede any **class** instruction (or any instruction that would start the default class).

If a program contains no **package** instruction then its package is implementation-defined. Typically it is grouped with other programs in some implementation-defined logical collection, such as a directory in a file system.

Examples:

```
package testpackage
package netrexx.process
```

When a class is identified as belonging to a package, it has a *qualified class name*, which is its short name, as given on the **class** instruction (see page 74), prefixed with the package name and a period. For example, if the short name of a class is "`RxLanguage`" and the package name is "`netrexx.process`" then the qualified name of the class would be "`netrexx.process.RxLanguage`".

In the reference implementation, packages are kept in a hierarchy derived from the Java classpath, where the segments of a package name correspond to a path in the hierarchy. The hierarchy is typically the directories in a file system, or some equivalent (such as a "Zip" archive file), and so package names should be considered case-sensitive (as some Java implementations use case-sensitive file systems).

SECTION 26: PARSE INSTRUCTION

> **parse** *term template* ;
>
> where *template* is one or more non-numeric *symbols* separated by blanks or *patterns*
>
> and a *pattern* is one of:
>
> *literalstring*
> [*indicator*] *number*
> [*indicator*] **(** *symbol* **)**
>
> and *indicator* is one of **+**, **–**, or **=**.

The **parse** instruction is used to assign characters (from a string) to one or more variables according to the rules and templates described in the section *Parsing templates* (see page 122).

The value of the *term* is expected to be a string; if it is not a string, it will be converted to a string.

Any variables used in the *template* are named by non-numeric *symbols* (that is, they cannot be an array reference or other term); they refer to a variable or property in the current class. Any values that are used in patterns during the parse are converted to strings before use.

Any variables set by the **parse** instruction must have a known string type, or are given the NetRexx string type, `Rexx`, if they are new.

The term itself is not changed unless it is a variable which also appears in the template and whose value is changed by being in the template.

Example:

```
parse wordlist word1 wordlist
```

In this idiomatic example, the first word is removed from `wordlist` and is assigned to the variable `word1`, and the remainder is assigned back to `wordlist`.

Notes:

1. The special words **ask**, **source**, and **version**, as described in the section *Special names and methods* (see page 118), allow:

   ```
   parse ask x     -- parses a line from input stream
   parse source x  -- parses 'Java method filename'
   parse version x -- parses 'NetRexx version date'
   ```

   These special words may also be used within expressions.

2. Similarly, it is recommended that the initial (main) method in a stand-alone application place the command string passed to it in a variable called `arg`.[42]

   If this is done, the instruction:

   ```
   parse arg template
   ```

   will work, in a stand-alone application, in the same way as in Rexx (even though `arg` is not a keyword in this case).[43]

SECTION 27: PROPERTIES INSTRUCTION

> **properties** [*visibility*] [*modifier*] ;
>
> where *visibility* is one of:
>
> **inheritable**
> **private**
> **public**
>
> and *modifier* is one of:
>
> **constant**
> **static**
> **volatile**
>
> and there must be at least one *visibility* or *modifier* keyword.

The **properties** instruction is used to define the attributes of following *property* variables, and therefore must precede the first **method** instruction in a class. A **properties** instruction replaces any previous **properties** instruction (that is, the attributes specified on **properties** instructions are not cumulative).

The *visibility* and *modifier* keywords may be in any order.

An example of the use of **properties** instructions may be found in the *Program Structure* section (see page 115).

Visibility

Properties may be **public**, **inheritable**, or **private**:

- A *public property* is visible to (that is, may be used by) all other classes to which the current class is visible.

---

42 *In the reference implementation, this is automatic if the* `main` *method is generated by the NetRexx language processor.*

43 Note, though, that the command string may have been edited by the environment; certain characters may not be allowed, multiple blanks may have been reduced to single blanks, *etc.*

- An *inheritable property* is visible to (that is, may be used by) only those classes that extend (that is, are subclasses of) or implement the current class.
- A *private property* is visible only within the current class.

By default, if no **properties** instruction is used, or *visibility* is not specified, properties are inheritable (but not public).[44]

Modifier

Properties may also be **constant**, **static**, or **volatile**:

- A *constant property* is associated with the class, rather than with an instance of the class (an object). It is initialized when the class is loaded and may not be changed thereafter.
- A *static property* is associated with the class, rather than with an instance of the class (an object). It is initialized when the class is loaded, and may be changed thereafter.
- A *volatile property* may change asynchronously, outside the control of the class, even when no method in the class is being executed. If an implementation does not allow asynchronous modification of properties, it should ignore this keyword.

Constant and static properties exist from when the class is first loaded (used), even if no object is constructed by the class, and there will only be one copy of each property. Other properties are constructed and initialized only when an object is constructed by the class; each object then has its own copy of such properties.

By default, if no **properties** instruction is used, or *modifier* is not specified, properties are associated with an object constructed by the class, and are neither constant nor volatile.

Properties in interface classes

In interface classes (see page 75), properties must be both **public** and **constant**. In such classes, these attributes for properties are the default and the **properties** instruction must not be used.

---

[44] The default, here, was chosen to encourage the "encapsulation" of data within classes.

SECTION 28: RETURN INSTRUCTION

return [*expression*];

return is used to return control (and possibly a result) from a NetRexx program or method to the point of its invocation.

The expression (if any) is evaluated, active control constructs are terminated (as though by a **leave** instruction), and the value of the expression is passed back to the caller.

The result passed back to the caller is a string of type `Rexx`, unless a different type was specified using the **returns** keyword on the **method** instruction (see page 93) for the current method. In this case, the type of the value of the expression must match (or be convertible to, as by the rules for assignment) the type specified by the **returns** phrase.

Within a method, the use of expressions on **return** must be consistent. That is, either all **return** instructions must specify a expression, or none may. If a **returns** phrase is given on the **method** instruction for the current method then all **return** instructions must specify an expression.

SECTION 29: SAY INSTRUCTION

say [*expression*];

say writes a string to the default output character stream. This typically causes it to be displayed (or spoken, or typed, *etc.*) to the user.

Example:

```
data=100
say data 'divided by 4 =>' data/4
/* would display:  "100 divided by 4 => 25"   */
```

The result of evaluating the *expression* is expected to be a string; if it is not a string, it will be converted to a string. This result string is written from the program via an implementation-defined output stream.

By default, the result string is treated as a "line" (an implementation-dependent mechanism for indicating line termination is effected after the string is written). If, however, the string ends in the NUL character (`'\-'` or `'\0'`) then that character is removed and line termination is not indicated.

The result string may be of any length. If no expression is specified, or the expression result is `null`, then an empty line is written (that is, as though the expression resulted in a null string).

SECTION 30: SELECT INSTRUCTION

> **select** [**label** *name*] [**protect** *termp*] ;
> *whenlist*
> [**otherwise** [;] *instructionlist*]
> [**catch** [*vare* =] *exception* ; *instructionlist*] ...
> [**finally** [;] *instructionlist*]
> **end** [*name*] ;
>
> where *name* is a non-numeric *symbol*
>
> and *whenlist* is one or more *whenconstructs*
>
> and *whenconstruct* is:
>
> **when** *expression* [;] **then** [;] *instruction*
>
> and *instructionlist* is zero or more *instructions*.

select is used to conditionally execute one of several alternatives. The construct may optionally be given a label, and may protect an object while the instructions in the construct are executed; exceptional conditions can be handled with **catch** and **finally**, which follow the body of the construct.

Each expression following a **when** is evaluated in turn and must result in either 0 or 1. If the result is 1, then the instruction following the associated **then** (which may be a complex instruction such as **if**, **do**, **loop**, or **select**) is executed and control will then pass directly to the **end**. If the result is 0, control will pass to the next **when** clause.

If none of the **when** expressions result in 1, then control will pass to the instruction list (if any) following **otherwise**. In this situation, the absence of an **otherwise** is a run-time error.[45]

Notes:

1. An *instruction* may be any assignment, method call, or keyword instruction, including any of the more complex constructions such as **do**, **loop**, **if**, and the **select** instruction itself. A null clause is not an instruction, however, so putting an extra semicolon after the **then** is not equivalent to putting a dummy instruction (as it would be in C or PL/I). The **nop** instruction is provided for this purpose.

2. The keyword **then** is treated specially, in that it need not start a clause. This allows the expression on the **when** clause to be terminated by the **then**, without a ";" being required – were this not so, people used to

---

[45] *In the reference implementation, a* `NoOtherwiseException` *is raised.*

other computer languages would be inconvenienced. Hence the symbol **then** cannot be used as a variable name within the expression.[46]

Label phrase

If **label** is used to specify a *name* for the select group, then a **leave** instruction (see page 84) which specifies that name may be used to leave the group, and the **end** that ends the group may optionally specify the name of the group for additional checking.

Example:

```
select label roman
  when a=b then say 'same'
  when a<b then say 'lo'
  otherwise
    say 'hi'
    if a=0 then leave roman
    say 'a non-0'
  end roman
```

In this example, if the variable a has the value 0 and b is non-zero then just "hi" is displayed.

Protect phrase

If **protect** is given it must be followed by a *term* that evaluates to a value that is not just a type and is not of a primitive type; while the **select** construct is being executed, the value (object) is protected – that is, all the instructions in the **select** construct have exclusive access to the object.

Both **label** and **protect** may be specified, in any order, if required.

Exceptions in select constructs

Exceptions that are raised by the instructions within the body of the group may be caught using one or more **catch** clauses that name the *exception* that they will catch. When an exception is caught, the exception object that holds the details of the exception may optionally be assigned to a variable, *vare*.

Similarly, a **finally** clause may be used to introduce instructions that will always be executed at the end of the select group, even if an exception is raised (whether caught or not).

The *Exceptions* section (see page 145) has details and examples of **catch** and **finally**.

---

46 Strictly speaking, **then** should only be recognized if not the name of a variable. In this special case, however, NetRexx language processors are permitted to treat **then** as reserved in the context of a **when** clause, to provide better performance and more useful error reporting.

SECTION 31: SIGNAL INSTRUCTION

> **signal** *term* ;

The **signal** instruction causes an "abnormal" change in the flow of control, by raising an *exception.*

The exception *term* may be a term that constructs or evaluates to an exception object, or it may be expressed as the name of an exception type (in which case the default constructor, with no arguments, for that type is used to construct an exception object). The exception object then represents the exception and is available, if required, when the exception is handled.

The handling of exceptions is detailed in the *Exceptions* section (see page 145). In summary, when an exception is signalled, all active pending **do** groups, **loop** loops, **if** constructs, and **select** constructs may be ended. For each one in turn, from the innermost:

1. No further clauses within the body of the construct will be executed (in this respect, **signal** acts like a **leave** for the construct).
2. The *instructionlist* following the first **catch** clause that matches the exception, if any, is executed.
3. The *instructionlist* following the **finally** clause for the construct, if any, is executed.

If a **catch** matched the exception the exception is deemed handled, and execution resumes as though the construct ended normally (unless a new exception was signalled in the **catch** or **finally** instruction lists, in which case it is processed). Otherwise, any enclosing construct is ended in the same manner. If there is no enclosing construct, then the current method is ended and the exception is signalled in the caller.

Examples:

```
signal RxErrorTrace
signal DivideException('Divide by zero')
```

In the reference implementation, the term must either

- *evaluate to an object that is assignable to the type* `Throwable` *(for example, a subclass of* `Exception` *or* `RuntimeException`*).*
- *be a type that is a subclass of* `Throwable`*, in which case the default constructor (with no arguments) for the given type is used to construct the exception object.*

SECTION 32: TRACE INSTRUCTION

```
        ┌ all     ┐
trace   │ methods │ ;
        │ off     │
        └ results ┘
```

The **trace** instruction is used to control the tracing of the execution of NetRexx methods, and is primarily used for debugging.

One **trace** instruction may appear before the first method in a class, in which case it sets the initial trace setting for all methods in the class (the default is **off**). Within methods, the **trace** instruction changes the trace setting when it is executed, and affects the tracing of all clauses in the method which are then executed (until changed by a later **trace** instruction).

trace all

All clauses (except null clauses without commentary) which are in methods and which are executed after the **trace** instruction will be traced. If **trace all** is placed before the first method in the current class, the **method** instructions in the class, together with the values of the arguments passed to each method, will be traced when the method is invoked (that is, **trace all** implies **trace methods**).

trace methods

All **method** clauses in the class will be traced when the method they introduce is invoked, together with the values of the arguments passed to each method; no other clauses, or results, will be traced. The **trace methods** instruction must be placed before the first method in the current class (as otherwise it would have no effect).

trace off

Turns tracing off; no following clauses, or results, will be traced.

trace results

All clauses (except null clauses without commentary) which are in methods and which are executed after the **trace** instruction will be traced, as though **trace all** had been requested. In addition, the results of all *expression* evaluations and any results assigned to a variable by an assignment, **loop**, or **parse** instruction are also traced.

If **trace results** is placed before the first method in the current class, the **method** instructions in the class will be traced when the method is invoked, together with the values of the arguments passed to each method.

Notes:

1. Tracing of clauses shows the data from the source of the program, starting at the first character of the first token of the clause and including any commentary from that point until the end of the clause.
2. When a loop is being traced, the **loop** clause itself will be traced on every iteration of the loop, as indicated by the programmer's model (see page 92); the **end** clause is only traced once, when the loop completes normally.
3. With **trace results**, an expression is not traced if it is immediately used for an assignment (in an assignment instruction, or when the control variable is initialized in a **loop** instruction). The assignment will trace the result of the expression.
4. Trace output is written to an implementation-defined output stream (typically the "standard error" output stream, which lets it be redirected to a destination separate from the default destination for output which is used by the **say** instruction).
5. In some implementations, the use of **trace** instructions may substantially increase the size of classes and the execution time of methods affected by tracing.[47]
6. With some implementations it may be possible to switch tracing on externally, without requiring modification to the program.

The format of trace output

Trace output is either clauses from the program being traced, or results (such as the results from expressions).

The first clause or result traced on any line will be preceded by its line number in the program; this is right-justified in a space which allows for the largest line number in the program, plus one blank. Following clauses or results from the same line are preceded by white space of the same width; however, any change of line number causes the line number to be included.

Clauses that are traced will be displayed with the formatting (indention) and layout used in the original source stream for the program, starting with the first character of the first token of the clause.

Results (if requested) are converted to a string for tracing if necessary, are not indented, and have a double quote prefixed and suffixed so that leading and trailing blanks are apparent; if, however, the result being traced is `null` (see page 119) then the string "`[null]`" is shown (without quotes). For results with an associated name (the values assigned to local variables,

---

[47] *In the reference implementation,* **options notrace** *may be used to disable all* **trace** *instructions and hence ensure that tracing overhead is not accidentally incurred.*

method arguments, or properties in the current class), the name of the result precedes the data, separated by a single blank.

For clarity, implementations may replace "control codes" in the encoding of results (for example, EBCDIC values less than '\x40', or Unicode values less than '\x20') by a question mark ("?").

All lines displayed during tracing have a three character tag to identify the type of data being traced. This tag follows the line number (or the space for a line number), and is separated from the line number by a single blank. The traced clause or result follows the tag, after another blank. The identifier tags may be:

`*=*` identifies the first line of the source of a single clause, *i.e.*, the data actually in the program.

`*-*` identifies a continuation line from the source of a single clause. Continuations may be due to the use of a continuation character (see page 37) or to the use of a block comment (see page 33) which spans more than one line.

`>a>` Identifies a value assigned to a method argument of the current method. The name of the argument is included in the trace.

`>p>` Identifies a value assigned to a property. The name of the property is included in the trace if the property is in the current class.

`>v>` Identifies a value assigned to a local variable in the current method. The name of the variable is included in the trace.

`>>>` Identifies the result of an expression evaluation that is not used for an assignment (for example, an argument expression in a method call).

`+++` Reserved for error messages that are not supplied by the environment underlying the implementation.

Examples:

If the following instructions, starting on line 53 of a 120-line program, were executed:

```
trace all
if i=1 then say 'Hello'
       else say 'i<>1'
say -
 'A continued line'
```

the trace output (if *i* were `1`) would be:

```
54 *=* if i=1
   *=*          then
   *=*                   say 'Hello'
56 *=* say -
57 *-*   'A continued line'
```

Similarly, for the 3-line program:

```
trace results
number=1/7
parse number before '.' after
```

the trace output would be:

```
 2 *=* number=1/7
   >v> number "0.142857143"
 3 *=* parse number before '.' after
   >v> before "0"
   >v> after "142857143"
```

SECTION 33: PROGRAM STRUCTURE

A NetRexx *program* is a collection of clauses (see page 32) derived from a single implementation-defined source stream (such as a file). When a program is processed by a language processor[48] it defines one or more classes. Classes are usually introduced by the **class** instruction (see page 74), but if the first is a standard class, intended to be run as a stand-alone application, then the **class** instruction can be omitted. In this case, NetRexx defines an implied class and initialization method that will be used.

The implied class and method permits the writing of "low boilerplate" programs, with a minimum of syntax. The simplest, documented, NetRexx program that has an effect might therefore be:

Example:

```
/* This is a very simple NetRexx program */
say 'Hello World!'
```

In more detail, a NetRexx program consists of:

1. An optional *prolog* (**package**, **import**, and **options** instructions). Only one **package** instruction is permitted per program.
2. One or more class definitions, each introduced by a **class** instruction.

A *class definition* comprises:

1. The **class** instruction which introduces the class (which may be inferred, see below).
2. Zero or more property variable assignments, along with optional **properties** instructions that can alter their attributes, and optional **numeric** and **trace** instructions. Property variable assignments take the form of an *assignment* (see page 65), with an optional "=" and expression, which may:
   - just name a property (by omitting the "=" and expression of the assignment), in which case it refers to a string of type `Rexx`
   - assign a type to the property (when the expression evaluates to just a type)
   - assign a type and initial value to the property (when the expression returns a value).
3. Zero or more method definitions, each introduced by a **method** instruction (which may be inferred if the **class** instruction is inferred, see below).

---

48 Such as a compiler or interpreter.

A *method definition* comprises:

- Any NetRexx instructions, except the **class**, **method**, and **properties** instructions and those allowed in the prolog (the **package**, **import**, and **options** instructions).

Example:

```
/* A program with two classes */
import java.applet.    -- for example

class testclass extends Applet
  properties public
    state                -- property of type 'Rexx'
    i=int                -- property of type 'int'
  properties constant
    j=int 3              -- property initialized to '3'

  method start
    say 'I started'
    state='start'

  method stop
    say 'I stopped'
    state='stop'

class anotherclass
  method testing
    loop i=1 to 10
      say '1, 2, 3, 4...'
      if i=7 then return
     end
    return

  method anothertest
    say '1, 2, 3, 4'
```

This example shows a prolog (with just an **import** instruction) followed by two classes. The first class includes two public properties, one constant property, and two methods. The second class includes no properties, but also has two methods.

Note that a **return** instruction implies no static scoping; the content of a method is ended by a **method** (or **class**) instruction, or by the end of the source stream. The **return** instruction at the end of the `testing` method is, therefore, unnecessary.

Program defaults

The following defaults are provided for NetRexx programs:

1. If, while parsing prolog instructions, some instruction that is not valid for the prolog and is not a **class** instruction is encountered, then a default **class** instruction (with an implementation-provided short name, typically derived from the name of the source stream) is inserted. If the instruction was not a **method** instruction, then a default **method** instruction (with a name and attributes appropriate for the environment, such as `main`) is also inserted.

   In this latter case, it is assumed that execution of the program will begin by invocation of the default method. In other words, a "stand-alone" application can be written without explicitly providing the class and method instructions for the first method to be executed. An example of such a program is given in Appendix B (see page 179).

   In the reference implementation, the `main` *method in a stand-alone application is passed the words forming the command string as an array of strings of type* `java.lang.String` *(one word to each element of the array). When the NetRexx reference implementation provides the* `main` *method instruction by default, it also constructs a NetRexx string of type* `Rexx` *from this array of words, with a blank added between words, and assigns the string to the variable* `arg`.

   The command string may also have been edited by the underlying operating system environment; certain characters may not be allowed, multiple blanks or whitespace may have been reduced to single blanks, etc.

2. If a method ends and the last instruction at the outer level of the method scope is not **return** then a **return** instruction is added if it could be reached. In this case, if a value is expected to be returned by the method (due to other **return** instructions returning values, or there being a **returns** keyword on the **method** instruction), an error is reported.

Language processors may provide options to prevent, or warn of, these defaults being applied, as desired.

SECTION 34: SPECIAL NAMES AND METHODS

For convenience, NetRexx provides some *special names* for naming commonly-used concepts within terms. These are only recognized if there is no variable of the same name previously seen in the current scope, as described in the section on *Terms* (see page 41). This allows the set of special words to be expanded in the future, if necessary, without invalidating existing variables. Therefore, these names are not reserved; they may be used as variable names instead, if desired.

There are also two "special methods" that are used when constructing objects.

Special names

The following special names are allowed in NetRexx programs, and are recognized independently of case.[49] With the exception of `length`, these may only be used alone as a term or at the start of a compound term.

`ask`

Returns a string of type `Rexx`, read as a line from the implementation-defined default input stream (often the user's "console").

Example:

```
if ask='yes' then say 'OK'
```

`ask` can only appear alone, or at the start of a compound term.[50]

`digits`

The current setting of **numeric digits** (see page 98), returned as a NetRexx string. This will be one or more arabic numerals, with no leading blanks or sign, and no trailing blanks or exponent.

`digits` can only appear alone, or at the start of a compound term.

`form`

The current setting of **numeric form** (see page 99), returned as a string of type `Rexx`. This will have either the value "`scientific`" or the value "`engineering`".

`form` can only appear alone, or at the start of a compound term.

---

49 *Unless* **options strictcase** *is in effect.*

50 *In the reference implementation,* `ask` *is simply a shorthand for* `RexxIO.Ask()`.

`length`

The length of an array (see page 71), returned as an implementation-dependent binary type or string. This word is only recognized as the last part of a compound term, where the evaluation of the rest of the term resulted in an array of dimension 1.

Example:

```
foo=char[7]
say foo.length     /* would say '7' */
```

Note that you can get the length of a NetRexx string with the same syntax.[51] In that case, however, a `length()` method is being invoked.

`null`

The *empty reference*. This is a special value that represents "no value" and may be assigned to variables (or returned from methods) except those whose type is both primitive and undimensioned. It may also be be used in a comparison for equality (or inequality) with values of suitable type, and may be given a type.

Examples:

```
blob=int[3]     -- 'blob' refers to array of 3 ints
blob=null       -- 'blob' is still of type int[],
                -- but refers to no real object
mob=Mark null -- 'mob' is type 'Mark'
```

The `null` value may be considered to represent the state of being uninitialized. It can only appear as simple symbol, not as a part of a compound term.

`source`

Returns a string of type `Rexx` identifying the source of the current class. The string consists of the following words, with a single blank between the words and no trailing or leading blanks:

1. the name of the underlying environment (*e.g.*, `Java`)
2. either `method` (if the term is being used within a method) or `class` (if the term is being used within a property assignment, before the first method in a class)
3. an implementation-dependent representation of the name of the source stream for the class (*e.g.*, `Fred.nrx`).

`source` can only appear alone, or at the start of a compound term.

---

51 *Unless* **options strictargs** *is in effect.*

`super`

Returns a reference to the current object, with a type that is the type of the class that the current object's class extends. This means that a search for methods or properties which `super` qualifies will start from the superclass rather than in the current class. This is used for invoking a method or property (in the superclass or one of its superclasses) that has been overridden in the current class.

Example:

```
method printit(x)
  say 'it'            -- modification
  super.printit(x)    -- now the usual processing
```

If a property being referenced is in fact defined by a superclass of the current class, then the prefix "`super.`" is perhaps the clearest way to indicate that name refers to a property of a superclass rather than to a local variable. (You could also qualify it by the name of the superclass.)

`super` can only appear alone, or at the start of a compound term.

`this`

Returns a reference to the current object. When a method is invoked, for example in:

```
word=Rexx "hello"   -- 'word' refers to "hello"
say word.substr(3)  -- invokes substr on "hello"
```

then the method `substr` in the class `Rexx` is invoked, with argument `'3'`, and with the properties of the value (object) `"hello"` available to it. These properties may be accessed simply by name, or (more explicitly) by prefixing the name with "`this.`". Using "`this.`" can make a method more readable, especially when several objects of the same type are being manipulated in the method.

`this` can only appear alone, or at the start of a compound term.

`trace`

The current **trace** (see page 111) setting, returned as a NetRexx string. This will be one of the words:

```
off methods all results
```

`trace` can only appear alone, or at the start of a compound term.

`version`

Returns a string of type `Rexx` identifying the version of the NetRexx language in effect when the current class was processed. The string consists of the following words, with a single blank between the words and no trailing or leading blanks:

1. A word describing the language. The first seven letters will be the characters `NetRexx`, and the remainder may be used to identify a particular implementation or language processor. This word may not include any periods.
2. The language level description, which must be a number with no sign or exponential part. For example, "`1.00`" is the language level of this definition.
3. Three words describing the language processor release date in the same format as the default for the Rexx "`date()`" function.[52] For example, "`7 Oct 1996`".

`version` can only appear alone, or at the start of a compound term.

Special methods

Constructors (methods used for constructing objects) in NetRexx must invoke a constructor of their superclass before making any modifications to the current object (or invoke another constructor in the current class).

This is simplified and made explicit by the provision of the special method names `super` and `this`, which refer to constructors of the superclass and current class respectively. These special methods are only recognized when used as the first, method call, instruction in a constructor, as described in *Methods and constructors* (see page 47). Their names will be recognized independently of case.[53]

In addition, NetRexx provides special constructor methods for the primitive types that allow binary construction of primitives. These are described in *Binary values and arithmetic* (see page 144).

---

[52] As defined in *American National Standard for Information Technology – Programming Language REXX, X3.274-1996*, American National Standards Institute, New York, 1996.

[53] *Unless* **options strictcase** *is in effect.*

SECTION 35: PARSING TEMPLATES

The **parse** instruction allows a selected string to be parsed (split up) and assigned to variables, under the control of a *template*.

The various mechanisms in the template allow a string to be split up by explicit matching of strings (called *patterns*), or by specifying numeric positions (*positional patterns* – for example, to extract data from particular columns of a line read from a character stream). Once split into parts, each segment of the string can then be assigned to variables as a whole or by words (delimited by blanks).

This section first gives some informal examples of how the parsing template can be used, and then defines the algorithms in detail.

Introduction to parsing

The simplest form of parsing template consists of a list of variable names. The string being parsed is split up into words (characters delimited by blanks), and each word from the string is assigned to a variable in sequence from left to right. The final variable is treated specially in that it will be assigned whatever is left of the original string and may therefore contain several words. For example, in the **parse** instruction:

```
parse 'This is a sentence.' v1 v2 v3
```

the term (in this case a literal string) following the instruction keyword is parsed, and then: the variable *v1* would be assigned the value "`This`", *v2* would be assigned the value "`is`", and *v3* would be assigned the value "`a sentence.`".

Leading blanks are removed from each word in the string before it is assigned to a variable, as is the blank that delimits the end of the word. Thus, variables set in this manner (*v1* and *v2* in the example) will never have leading or trailing blanks, though *v3* could have both leading and trailing blanks.

Note that the variables assigned values in a template are always given a new value and so if there are fewer words in the string than variables in the template then the unused variables will be set to the null string.

The second parsing mechanism uses a literal string in a template as a pattern, to split up the string. For example:

```
parse 'To be, or not to be?' w1 ',' w2
```

would cause the string to be scanned for the comma, and then split at that point; the variable *w1* would be set to "`To be`", and *w2* is set to "` or not to be?`". Note that the pattern itself (and **only** the pattern) is removed from the string. Each section of the string is treated in just the same way as the whole string was in the previous example, and so either section could be split up into words.

Thus, in:

```
parse 'To be, or not to be?' w1 ',' w2 w3 w4
```

w2 and *w3* would be assigned the values “or” and “not”, and *w4* would be assigned the remainder: “to be?”.

If the string in the last example did not contain a comma, then the pattern would effectively “match” the end of the string, so the variable to the left of the pattern would get the entire input string, and the variables to the right would be set to a null string.

The pattern may be specified as a variable, by putting the variable name in parentheses. The following instructions therefore have the same effect as the last example:

```
c=','
parse 'To be, or not to be?' w1 (c) w2 w3 w4
```

The third parsing mechanism is the numeric positional pattern. This works in the same way as the string pattern except that it specifies a column number. So:

```
parse 'Flying pigs have wings' x1 5 x2
```

would split the string at the fifth column, so *x1* would be “Flyi” and *x2* would start at column 5 and so be “ng pigs have wings”.

More than one pattern is allowed, so for example:

```
parse 'Flying pigs have wings' x1 5 x2 10 x3
```

would split the string at columns 5 and 10, so *x2* would be “ng pi” and *x3* would be “gs have wings”.

The numbers can be relative to the last number used, so:

```
parse 'Flying pigs have wings' x1 5 x2 +5 x3
```

would have exactly the same effect as the last example; here the +5 may be thought of as specifying the length of the string to be assigned to *x2*.

As with literal string patterns, the positional patterns can be specified as a variable by putting the name of a variable, in parentheses, in place of the number. An absolute column number should then be indicated by using an equals sign (“=”) instead of a plus or minus sign. The last example could therefore be written:

```
start=5
length=5
data='Flying pigs have wings'
parse data  x1 =(start) x2 +(length) x3
```

String patterns and positional patterns can be mixed (in effect the beginning of a string pattern just specifies a variable column number) and some very powerful things can be done with templates. The next section describes in more detail how the various mechanisms interact.

Parsing definition

This section describes the rules that govern parsing.

In its most general form, a template consists of alternating pattern specifications and variable names. Blanks may be added between patterns and variable names to separate the tokens and to improve readability. The patterns and variable names are used strictly in sequence from left to right, and are used once only. In practice, various simpler forms are used in which either variable names or patterns may be omitted; we can therefore have variable names without patterns in between, and patterns without intervening variable names.

In general, the value assigned to a variable is that sequence of characters in the input string between the point that is matched by the pattern on its left and the point that is matched by the pattern on its right.

If the first item in a template is a variable, then there is an implicit pattern on the left that matches the start of the string, and similarly if the last item in a template is a variable then there is an implicit pattern on the right that matches the end of the string. Hence the simplest template consists of a single variable name which in this case is assigned the entire input string.

Setting a variable during parsing is identical in effect to setting a variable in an assignment.

The constructs that may appear as patterns fall into two categories; patterns that act by searching for a matching string (literal patterns), and numeric patterns that specify an absolute or relative position in the string (positional patterns). Either of these can be specified explicitly in the template, or alternatively by a reference to a variable whose value is to be used as the pattern.

For the following examples, assume that the following sample string is being parsed; note that all blanks are significant – there are two blanks after the first word "is" and also after the second comma:

```
'This is  the text which, I think,  is scanned.'
```

Parsing with literal patterns

Literal patterns cause scanning of the data string to find a sequence that matches the value of the literal. Literals are expressed as a quoted string. The null string matches the end of the data.

The template:

```
w1 ',' w2 ',' w3
```

when parsing the sample string, results in:

w1 has the value `"This is  the text which"`
w2 has the value `" I think"`
w3 has the value `"  is scanned."`

Here the string is parsed using a template that asks that each of the variables receive a value corresponding to a portion of the original string between commas; the commas are given as quoted strings. Note that the patterns themselves are removed from the data being parsed.

A different parse would result with the template:

```
w1 ',' w2 ',' w3 ',' w4
```

which would result in:

w1 has the value `"This is  the text which"`
w2 has the value `" I think"`
w3 has the value `"  is scanned."`
w4 has the value `""  (null string)`

This illustrates an important rule. When a match for a pattern cannot be found in the input string, it instead "matches" the end of the string. Thus, no match was found for the third `','` in the template, and so *w3* was assigned the rest of the string. *w4* was assigned a null string because the pattern on its left had already reached the end of the string.

Note that **all** variables that appear in a template in this way are assigned a new value.

Parsing strings into words

If a variable is directly followed by one or more other variables, then the string selected by the patterns is assigned to the variables in the following manner. Each blank-delimited word in the string is assigned to each variable in turn, except for the last variable in the group (which is assigned the remainder of the string). The values of the variables which are assigned words will have neither leading nor trailing blanks.

Thus the template:

```
w1 w2 w3 w4 ','
```

would result in:

w1 has the value "This'
w2 has the value "is"
w3 has the value "the"
w4 has the value "text which"

Note that the final variable (*w4* in this example) could have had both leading blanks and trailing blanks, since only the blank that delimits the previous word is removed from the data.

Also observe that this example is not the same as specifying explicit blanks as patterns, as the template:

```
w1 ' ' w2 ' ' w3 ' ' w4 ','
```

would in fact result in:

w1 has the value "This'
w2 has the value "is"
w3 has the value "" (null string)
w4 has the value "the text which"

since the third pattern would match the third blank in the data.

In general, when a variable is followed by another variable then parsing of the input into individual words is implied. The parsing process may be thought of as first splitting the original string up into other strings using the various kinds of patterns, and then assigning each of these new strings to (zero or more) variables.

Use of the period as a placeholder

A period (separated from any symbols by at least one blank) acts as a placeholder in a template. It has exactly the same effect as a variable name, except that no variable is set. It is especially useful as a "dummy variable" in a list of variables, or to collect (ignore) unwanted information at the end of a string. Thus the template:

```
. . . word4 .
```

would extract the fourth word ("`text`") from the sample string and place it in the variable *word4*. Blanks between successive periods in templates may be omitted, so the template:

```
... word4 .
```

would have the same result as the last template.

Parsing with positional patterns

Positional patterns may be used to cause the parsing to occur on the basis of position within the string, rather than on its contents. They take the form of whole numbers, optionally preceded by a plus, minus, or equals sign which indicate relative or absolute positioning. These may cause the matching operation to "back up" to an earlier position in the data string, which can only occur when positional patterns are used.

Absolute positional patterns: A number in a template that is **not** preceded by a sign refers to a particular (absolute) character column in the input, with 1 referring to the first column. For example, the template:

```
s1 10 s2 20 s3
```

results in:

s1 has the value `"This is  "`
s2 has the value `"the text w"`
s3 has the value `"hich, I think,  is scanned."`

Here *s1* is assigned characters from the first through the ninth character, and *s2* receives input characters 10 through 19. As usual the final variable, *s3*, is assigned the remainder of the input.

An equals sign ("=") may be placed before the number to indicate explicitly that it is to be used as an absolute column position; the last template could have been written:

```
s1 =10 s2 =20 s3
```

A positional pattern that has no sign or is preceded by the equals sign is known as an *absolute positional pattern.*

Relative positional patterns: A number in a template that is preceded by a plus or minus sign indicates movement relative to the character position at which the previous pattern match occurred. This is a *relative positional pattern.*

If a plus or minus is specified, then the position used for the next match is calculated by adding (or subtracting) the number given to the last matched position. The last matched position is the position of the first character of the last match, whether specified numerically or by a string.

For example, the instructions:

```
parse '123456789'  3 w1 +3 w2 3 w3
```

result in

w1 has the value `"345"`
w2 has the value `"6789"`
w3 has the value `"3456789"`

The +3 in this case is equivalent to the absolute number 6 in the same position, and may also be considered to be specifying the length of the data string to be assigned to the variable *w1*.

This example also illustrates the effects of a positional pattern that implies movement to a character position to the left of (or to) the point at which the last match occurred. The variable on the left is assigned characters through the end of the input, and the variable on the right is, as usual, assigned characters starting at the position dictated by the pattern.

A useful effect of this is that multiple assignments can be made:

```
parse x 1 w1 1 w2 1 w3
```

This results in assigning the (entire) value of *x* to *w1*, *w2*, and *w3*. (The first "1" here could be omitted as it is effectively the same as the implicit starting pattern described at the beginning of this section.)

If a positional pattern specifies a column that is greater than the length of the data, it is equivalent to specifying the end of the data (*i.e.*, no padding takes place). Similarly, if a pattern specifies a column to the left of the first column of the data, this is not an error but instead is taken to specify the first column of the data.

Any pattern match sets the "last position" in a string to which a relative positional pattern can refer. The "last position" set by a literal pattern is the position at which the match occurred, that is, the position in the data of the *first* character in the pattern. The literal pattern in this case is **not** removed from the parsed data. Thus the template:

```
',' -1 x +1
```

will:

1. Find the first comma in the input (or the end of the string if there is no comma).
2. Back up one position.
3. Assign one character (the character immediately preceding the comma or end of string) to the variable *x*.

One possible application of this is looking for abbreviations in a string. Thus the instruction:

```
/* Ensure options have a leading blank and are
   in uppercase before parsing. */
parse (' 'opts).upper ' PR' +1 prword ' '
```

will set the variable *prword* to the first word in *opts* that starts with "PR" (in any case), or will set it to the null string if no such word exists.

Notes:

1. The positional patterns +0 and -0 are valid, have the same effect, and may be used to include the whole of a previous literal (or variable) pattern within the data string to be parsed into any following variables.
2. As illustrated in the last example, patterns may follow each other in the template without intervening variable names. In this case each pattern is obeyed in turn from left to right, as usual.
3. There may be blanks between the sign in a positional pattern and the number, because NetRexx defines that blanks adjacent to special characters are removed.

Parsing with variable patterns

It is sometimes desirable to be able to specify a pattern by using the value of a variable instead of a fixed string or number. This may be achieved by placing the name of the variable to be used as the pattern in parentheses (blanks are not necessary either inside or outside the parentheses, but may be added if desired). This is called a *variable reference*; the value of the variable is converted to string before use, if necessary.

If the parenthesis to the left of the variable name is not preceded by an equals, plus, or minus sign ("=", "+", or "-") the value of the variable is then used as though it were a literal (string) pattern. The variable may be one that has been set earlier in the parsing process, so for example:

```
input="L/look for/1 10"
parse input  verb 2 delim +1 string (delim) rest
```

will set:

verb to 'L'
delim to '/'
string to 'look for'
rest to '1 10'

If the left parenthesis **is** preceded by an equals, plus, or minus sign then the value of the variable is used as an absolute or relative positional pattern (instead of as a literal string pattern). In this case the value of the variable must be a non-negative whole number, and (as before) it may have been set earlier in the parsing process.

SECTION 36: NUMBERS AND ARITHMETIC

NetRexx arithmetic attempts to carry out the usual operations (including addition, subtraction, multiplication, and division) in as "natural" a way as possible. What this really means is that the rules followed are those that are conventionally taught in schools and colleges. However, it was found that unfortunately the rules used vary considerably (indeed much more than generally appreciated) from person to person and from application to application and in ways that are not always predictable. The NetRexx arithmetic described here is therefore a compromise which (although not the simplest) should provide acceptable results in most applications.

Introduction

Numbers can be expressed in NetRexx very flexibly (leading and trailing blanks are permitted, exponential notation may be used) and follow conventional syntax. Some valid numbers are:

```
     12          /* A whole number                 */
   '-76'         /* A signed whole number          */
     12.76       /* Some decimal places            */
 ' +  0.003 '    /* Blanks around the sign, etc.  */
     17.         /* Equal to 17                    */
      '.5'       /* Equal to 0.5                   */
     4E+9        /* Exponential notation           */
      0.73e-7    /* Exponential notation           */
```

(Exponential notation means that the number includes a sign and a power of ten following an "E" that indicates how the decimal point will be shifted. Thus `4E+9` above is just a short way of writing `4000000000`, and `0.73e-7` is short for `0.000000073`.)

The arithmetic operators include addition (indicated by a "+"), subtraction ("-"), multiplication ("*"), power ("**"), and division ("/"). There are also two further division operators: integer divide ("%") which divides and returns the integer part, and remainder ("//") which divides and returns the remainder. Prefix plus ("+") and prefix minus ("-") operators are also provided.

When two numbers are combined by an operation, NetRexx uses a set of rules to define what the result will be (and how the result is to be represented as a character string). These rules are defined in the next section, but in summary:

- Results will be calculated with up to some maximum number of significant digits. That is, if a result required more than 9 digits it would normally be rounded to 9 digits. For instance, the division of 2 by 3 would result in 0.666666667 (it would require an infinite number of digits for perfect accuracy).

You can change the default of 9 significant digits by using the **numeric digits** instruction. This lets you calculate using however many digits that you need – thousands, if necessary.

- Except for the power and division operators, trailing zeros are preserved (this is in contrast to most electronic calculators, which remove all trailing zeros in the decimal part of results). So, for example:

```
2.40 + 2  =>  4.40
2.40 - 2  =>  0.40
2.40 * 2  =>  4.80
2.40 / 2  =>  1.2
```

This preservation of trailing zeros is desirable for most calculations (and especially financial calculations).

If necessary, trailing zeros may be easily removed with the `strip` method (see page 164), or by division by 1.

- A zero result is always expressed as the single digit `'0'`.
- Exponential form is used for a result depending on its value and the setting of **numeric digits** (the default is 9 digits). If the number of places needed before the decimal point exceeds this setting, or the absolute value of the number is less than `0.000001`, then the number will be expressed in exponential notation; thus

```
1e+6 * 1e+6
```

results in "`1E+12`" instead of "`1000000000000`", and

```
1 / 3E10
== 3.33333333E-11
```

results in "`3.33333333E-11`" instead of "`0.0000000000333333333`".

- Any mixture of arabic numerals (0-9) and Extra digits (see page 35) can be used for the digits in numbers used in calculations. The results are expressed using arabic numerals.

Definition

This definition describes arithmetic for NetRexx strings (type `Rexx`). The arithmetic operations are identical to those defined in the ANSI standard for Rexx.[54]

Numbers

A *number* in NetRexx is a character string that includes one or more decimal digits, with an optional decimal point. The decimal point may be embedded in the digits, or may be prefixed or suffixed to them. The group of digits (and optional point) thus constructed may have leading or trailing blanks, and an optional sign ("+" or "–") which must come before any digits or decimal point. The sign may also have leading or trailing blanks. Thus:

```
sign    ::=  + | -
digit   ::=  0 | 1 | 2 | 3 | 4 | 5 | 6 | 7 | 8 | 9
digits  ::=  digit [digit]...
numeric ::=  digits . [digits]
             | [.] digits
number  ::=  [blank]... [sign [blank]...]
             numeric [blank]...
```

where if the implementation supports extra digits (see page 35) these are also accepted as *digits*, providing that they represent values in the range zero through nine. In this case each extra digit is treated as though it were the corresponding character in the range 0-9.

Note that a single period alone is not a valid number.

Precision

The maximum number of significant digits that can result from an arithmetic operation is controlled by the **digits** keyword on the **numeric** instruction (see page 98):

numeric digits [*expression*];

The expression is evaluated and must result in a positive whole number. This defines the precision (number of significant digits) to which arithmetic calculations will be carried out; results will be rounded to that precision, if necessary.

If no expression is specified, then the default precision is used. The default precision is 9, that is, all implementations must support at least nine digits of precision. An implementation-dependent maximum (equal to or larger than 9) may apply: an attempt to exceed this will cause execution of the

---

54 *American National Standard for Information Technology – Programming Language REXX, X3.274-1996*, American National Standards Institute, New York, 1996.

instruction to terminate with an exception. Thus if an algorithm is defined to use more than 9 digits then if the **numeric digits** instruction succeeds then the computation will proceed and produce identical results to any other implementation.

Note that **numeric digits** may set values below the default of nine. Small values, however, should be used with care – the loss of precision and rounding thus requested will affect all NetRexx computations, including (for example) the computation of new values for the control variable in loops.

In the remainder of this section, the notation `digits` refers to the current setting of **numeric digits**. This setting may also be referred to in expressions in programs by using the `digits` special word (see page 118).

Arithmetic operators

NetRexx arithmetic is effected by the operators "+", "–", "*", "/", "%", "//", and "**" (add, subtract, multiply, divide, integer divide, remainder, and power) which all act upon two terms, together with the prefix operators "+" and "–" (plus and minus) which both act on a single term. The result of all these operations is a NetRexx string, of type `Rexx`. This section describes the way in which these operations are carried out.

Before every arithmetic operation, the term or terms being operated upon have any extra digits converted to the corresponding arabic numeral (the digits 0-9). They then have leading zeros removed (noting the position of any decimal point, and leaving just one zero if all the digits in the number are zeros) and are then truncated to `digits+1` significant digits[55] (if necessary) before being used in the computation. The operation is then carried out under up to double that precision, as described under the individual operations below. When the operation is completed, the result is rounded if necessary to the precision specified by the **numeric digits** instruction.

Rounding is done in the "traditional" manner, in that the extra (guard) digit is inspected and values of 5 through 9 are rounded up, and values of 0 through 4 are rounded down.[56]

A conventional zero is supplied preceding a decimal point if otherwise there would be no digit before it. Trailing zeros are retained for addition, subtraction, and multiplication, according to the rules given below, except that a result of zero is always expressed as the single character `'0'`. For division, insignificant trailing zeros are removed after rounding.

The `format` method (see page 156) is defined to allow a number to be represented in a particular format if the standard result provided by NetRexx does not meet requirements.

---

55 That is, to the precision set by **numeric digits**, plus one extra "guard" digit.

56 Even/odd rounding would require the ability to calculate to arbitrary precision (that is, to a precision not governed by the setting of **numeric digits**) at any time and is therefore not the mechanism defined for NetRexx.

Arithmetic operation rules – basic operators

The basic operators (addition, subtraction, multiplication, and division) operate on numbers as follows:

Addition and subtraction

If either number is zero then the other number, rounded to `digits` digits if necessary, is used as the result (with sign adjustment as appropriate). Otherwise, the two numbers are extended on the right and left as necessary up to a total maximum of `digits+1` digits.

The number with smaller absolute value may therefore lose some or all of its digits on the right.[57] The numbers are then added or subtracted as appropriate. For example:

```
xxxx.xxx + yy.yyyyy
```

becomes:

```
   xxxx.xxx00
 + 00yy.yyyyy
 ------------
   zzzz.zzzzz
```

The result is then rounded to `digits` digits if necessary, taking into account any extra (carry) digit on the left after an addition, but otherwise counting from the position corresponding to the most significant digit of the terms being added or subtracted. Finally, any insignificant leading zeros are removed.

The *prefix operators* are evaluated using the same rules; the operations "`+number`" and "`-number`" are calculated as "`0+number`" and "`0-number`", respectively.

Multiplication

The numbers are multiplied together ("long multiplication") resulting in a number which may be as long as the sum of the lengths of the two operands. For example:

```
xxx.xxx * yy.yyyyy
```

becomes:

```
zzzzz.zzzzzzzz
```

and the result is then rounded to `digits` digits if necessary, counting from the first significant digit of the result.

---

57 In the example, the number `yy.yyyyy` would have three digits truncated if `digits` were `5`.

Division

For the division:

```
yyy / xxxxx
```

the following steps are taken: first, the number "yyy" is extended with zeros on the right until it is larger than the number "xxxxx" (with note being taken of the change in the power of ten that this implies). Thus in this example, "yyy" might become "yyy00". Traditional long division then takes place, which can be written:

```
         zzzz
xxxxx ) yyy00
```

The length of the result ("zzzz") is such that the rightmost "z" will be at least as far right as the rightmost digit of the (extended) "y" number in the example. During the division, the "y" number will be extended further as necessary, and the "z" number (which will not include any leading zeros) may increase up to digits+1 digits, at which point the division stops and the result is rounded. Following completion of the division (and rounding if necessary), insignificant trailing zeros are removed.

Examples:

```
/* With 'numeric digits 5' */
12+7.00      ==  19.00
1.3-1.07     ==  0.23
1.3-2.07     ==  -0.77
1.20*3       ==  3.60
7*3          ==  21
0.9*0.8      ==  0.72
1/3          ==  0.33333
2/3          ==  0.66667
5/2          ==  2.5
1/10         ==  0.1
12/12        ==  1
8.0/2        ==  4
```

Note: With all the basic operators, the position of the decimal point in the terms being operated upon is arbitrary. The operations may be carried out as integer operations with the exponent being calculated and applied afterwards. Therefore the significant digits of a result are not in any way dependent on the position of the decimal point in either of the terms involved in the operation.

Arithmetic operation rules – additional operators

The operation rules for the power ("`**`"), integer divide ("`%`"), and remainder ("`//`") operators are as follows:

Power

The "`**`" (power) operator raises a number (on the left of the operator) to a power (on the right of the operator). The term on the right is rounded to `digits` digits (if necessary), and must, after any rounding, be a whole number, which may be positive, negative, or zero. If negative, the absolute value of the power is used, and then the result is inverted (divided into 1).

For calculating the power, the number is effectively multiplied by itself for the number of times expressed by the power, and finally trailing zeros are removed (as though the result were divided by one).

In practice (see note below for the reasons), the power is calculated by the process of left-to-right binary reduction. For "`x**n`": "`n`" is converted to binary, and a temporary accumulator is set to 1. If "`n`" has the value 0 then the initial calculation is complete. Otherwise each bit (starting at the first non-zero bit) is inspected from left to right. If the current bit is 1 then the accumulator is multiplied by "`x`". If all bits have now been inspected then the initial calculation is complete, otherwise the accumulator is squared and the next bit is inspected for multiplication. When the initial calculation is complete, the temporary result is divided into 1 if the power was negative.

The multiplications and division are done under the normal arithmetic operation rules, detailed earlier in this section, using a precision of `digits+elength+1` digits. Here, `elength` is the length in digits of the integer part of the whole number "`n`" (*i.e.*, excluding any decimal part, decimal point, or insignificant leading zeros, as though the operation `n%1` had been carried out). Finally, the result is rounded to `digits` digits, if necessary, and insignificant trailing zeros are removed.

Integer division

The "`%`" (integer divide) operator divides two numbers and returns the integer part of the result. The result returned is defined to be that which would result from repeatedly subtracting the divisor from the dividend while the dividend is larger than the divisor. During this subtraction, the absolute values of both the dividend and the divisor are used: the sign of the final result is the same as that which would result if normal division were used.

The result returned will have no fractional part (that is, no decimal point or zeros following it). If the result cannot be expressed exactly within `digits` digits, the operation is in error and will fail – that is, the result cannot have more digits than the current setting of **numeric digits**. For example, `10000000000%3` requires 10 digits to express the result exactly (3333333333) and would therefore fail if digits were 9 or less.

Remainder

The "//" (remainder) operator will return the remainder from integer division, and is defined as being the residue of the dividend after the operation of calculating integer division as just described. The sign of the remainder, if non-zero, is the same as that of the original dividend.

This operation will fail under the same conditions as integer division (that is, if integer division on the same two terms would fail, the remainder cannot be calculated).

Examples:

```
/* Again with 'numeric digits 5' */
2**3         ==  8
2**-3        ==  0.125
1.7**8       ==  69.758
2%3          ==  0
2.1//3       ==  2.1
10%3         ==  3
10//3        ==  1
-10//3       ==  -1
10.2//1      ==  0.2
10//0.3      ==  0.1
3.6//1.3     ==  1.0
```

Notes:

1. A particular algorithm for calculating powers is described, since it is efficient (though not optimal) and considerably reduces the number of actual multiplications performed. It therefore gives better performance than the simpler definition of repeated multiplication. Since results could possibly differ from those of repeated multiplication, the algorithm must be defined here so that different implementations will give identical results for the same operation on the same values. Other algorithms for this (and other) operations may always be used, so long as they give identical results to those described here.

2. The integer divide and remainder operators are defined so that they may be calculated as a by-product of the standard division operation (described above). The division process is ended as soon as the integer result is available; the residue of the dividend is the remainder.

Numeric comparisons

Any of the comparative operators (see page 58) may be used for comparing numeric strings. However, the strict comparisons (for example, "==" and ">>") are not numeric comparative operators and should not normally be used for comparing numbers, since they compare from left to right and leading and trailing blanks (and leading zeros) are significant for these operators.

Numeric comparison, using the normal comparative operators, is effected by subtracting the two numbers (calculating the difference) and then comparing the result with `'0'` – that is, the operation:

```
A ? B
```

where "?" is any normal comparative operator, is identical to:

```
(A - B) ? '0'
```

It is therefore the *difference* between two numbers, when subtracted under NetRexx subtraction rules, that determines their equality.

Exponential notation

The definition of numbers above (see page 132) describes "pure" numbers, in the sense that the character strings that describe numbers can be very long.

Examples:

```
say  10000000000 * 10000000000
/* would display: 100000000000000000000 */

say  0.00000000001 * 0.00000000001
/* would display: 0.0000000000000000000001 */
```

For both large and small numbers some form of exponential notation is useful, both to make such long numbers more readable and to make execution possible in extreme cases. In addition, exponential notation is used whenever the "pure" form would give misleading information. For example:

```
numeric digits 5
say 54321*54321
```

would display "`2950800000`" if long form were to be used. This is misleading, and so NetRexx would express the result in exponential notation, in this case "`2.9508E+9`".

The definition of *numbers* (see above) is therefore extended by replacing the description of `numeric` by the following:

```
mantissa ::=  digits . [digits]
              | [.] digits
numeric  ::=  mantissa [E sign digits]
```

In other words, the numeric part of a number may be followed by an "E" (indicating an exponential part), a sign, and an integer following the sign that represents a power of ten that is to be applied. The "E" may be in uppercase or lowercase. Note that no blanks are permitted within this part of a number.

Examples:

```
12E+11  =  1200000000000
12E-5   =  0.00012
 12e+4  =  120000
```

All valid numbers may be used as data for arithmetic. The results of calculations will be returned in exponential form depending on the setting of **numeric digits**. If the number of places needed before the decimal point exceeds `digits`, or if the absolute value of the result is less than `0.000001`, then exponential form will be used. The exponential form generated by NetRexx always has a sign following the "E". If the exponent is 0 then the exponential part is omitted – that is, an exponential part of "E+0" will never be generated.

If the default format for a number is not satisfactory for a particular application, then the `format` method may be used to control its format. Using this, numbers may be explicitly converted to exponential form or even forced to be returned in "pure" form.

Different exponential notations may be selected with the **numeric form** instruction (see page 99). This instruction allows the selection of either scientific or engineering notation. Scientific notation adjusts the power of ten so there is a single non-zero digit to the left of the decimal point. Engineering notation causes powers of ten to be expressed as a multiple of three – the integer part may therefore range from `1` through `999`.

Examples:

```
numeric form scientific
say 123.45 * 1e11
/* would display: 1.2345E+13 */

numeric form engineering
say 123.45  * 1e11
/* would display: 12.345E+12 */
```

The default exponential notation is scientific.

Whole numbers

Within the set of numbers understood by NetRexx it is useful to distinguish the subset defined as *whole numbers.*

A *whole number* in NetRexx is a number that has a decimal part which is all zeros (or that has no decimal part).

Numbers used directly by NetRexx

As discussed above, the result of any arithmetic operation is rounded (if necessary) according to the setting of **numeric digits**. Similarly, when a number (which has not necessarily been involved in an arithmetic operation) is used directly by NetRexx then the same rounding is also applied, just as though the operation of adding the number to 0 had been carried out.

In the following cases, the number used must be a whole number and an implementation restriction on the largest number that can be used may apply:

- positional patterns, including variable positional patterns, in parsing templates (see page 122)
- the power value (right hand operand) of the power operator (see page 136)
- the values of *exprr* and *exprf* (following the **for** keyword) in the **loop** instruction (see page 85)
- the value of *exprd* (following the **digits** keyword) in the **numeric** instruction (see page 98).

Implementation minimum: A minimum length of 9 digits must be supported for these uses of whole numbers by a NetRexx language processor.

Implementation independence

The NetRexx arithmetic rules are defined in detail, so that when a given program is run the results of all computations are sufficiently defined that the same answer will result for all correct implementations. Differences due to the underlying machine architecture will not affect computations.

This contrasts with most other programming languages, and with binary arithmetic (see page 142) in NetRexx, where the result obtained may depend on the implementation because the precision and algorithms used by the language processor are defined by the implementation rather than by the language.

Exceptions and errors

The following exceptions and errors may be signalled during arithmetic:

- Divide exception

  This exception will be signalled if division by zero was attempted, or if the integer result of an integer divide or remainder operation had too many digits.

- Overflow/Underflow exception

  This exception will be signalled if the exponential part of a result (from an operation that is not an attempt to divide by zero) would exceed the range that can be handled by the language processor, when the result is formatted according to the current settings of **numeric digits** and **numeric form**. The language defines a minimum capability for the exponential part, namely exponents whose absolute value is at least as large as the largest number that can be expressed as an exact integer in default precision. Thus, since the default precision is nine, implementations must support exponents in the range `-999999999` through `999999999`.

- Insufficient storage

  Storage is needed for calculations and intermediate results, and on occasion an arithmetic operation may fail due to lack of storage. This is considered an operating environment error as usual, rather than an arithmetical exception.

In the reference implementation, the exceptions and error types used for these three cases are `DivideException`, `ExponentOverflowException`, *and* `OutOfMemoryError`, *respectively.*

SECTION 37: BINARY VALUES AND OPERATIONS

By default, arithmetic and string operations in NetRexx are carried out using the NetRexx string class, `Rexx`, which offers the robust set of operators described in *Expressions and operators* (see page 56).

NetRexx implementations, however, may also provide *primitive* datatypes, as described in *Types and Classes* (see page 39). These primitive types are used for compact storage of numbers and for fast binary arithmetic, features which are built-in to the hardware of most computers.

To make use of binary arithmetic, a class is declared to be a *binary class* (see page 76) by using the **binary** keyword on the **class** instruction. In such a class, literal strings and numeric symbols are assigned native string or primitive types, rather than NetRexx types, where appropriate, and native binary operations are used to implement operators where possible, as detailed below. Implementations may also provide a keyword on the **options** (see page 100) instruction that indicates that all classes in a program are binary classes.[58]

Binary classes should be used with care. Although binary arithmetic can have a considerable performance advantage over arithmetic that is not implemented in hardware, it can give incorrect or unexpected results. In particular, whole numbers (integers) are often held in fixed-sized data areas (of 8, 16, 32, or 64 bits), and overflowing the data area during a calculation can result in a positive number becoming negative and vice versa. Similarly, binary numbers that are not whole numbers (floating-point numbers) cannot exactly represent common numbers in the decimal system (`0.1`, `0.2`, *etc.*), and hence can give unexpected results.

Operations in binary classes

In a binary class, the following (and only the following) rules differ from the rules for other classes:

Dyadic operations in expressions

If the operands of a dyadic operator both have primitive numeric types[59] then binary operations are carried out. The type of the result is implementation defined, and is typically the type of the more precise of the two operands, or of some minimum precision.[60] Arithmetic oper-

---

58 *In the reference implementation,* **options binary** *is used.*

59 *In the reference implementation,* `boolean` *is considered to be a numeric type (having the values* `0` *or* `1`*) but* `char` *is not. Characters, and strings or arrays of characters, always use the rules defined for NetRexx strings.*

60 *In the reference implementation, the minimum precision is 32 bits, so an* `int` *is returned for results that would otherwise be* `byte` *or* `short`*. If both operands are* `boolean`*, however, and the operation is a logical operation, then the type of the result is* `boolean`*.*

ations follow the usual rules of binary arithmetic, as defined for the underlying environment of the implementation.

Note that NetRexx provides both divide and integer divide operators; in a binary class, the divide operator ("/") converts its operands to floating-point types and returns a floating-point result, whereas the integer divide operator ("%") converts its operands to integer types and returns an integer result. The remainder operator must accept both integer and floating-point types.

Logical operations (*and*, *or*, and *exclusive or*) apply to all the bits of the operands, and are not permitted on floating-point types.

Prefix operations in expressions

If the operand of a prefix operator has a primitive numeric type, then the type of the result is the type of the operand, subject to the same minimum as dyadic operations. Prefix plus and minus follow the rules of dyadic operators (because they are defined as being zero plus or minus the operand) with the additional rule that if acting on a literal number (a constant in the program) then the result is also considered to be a literal constant. Logical not (prefix "\") does not apply to all the bits of its operand; instead, it changes a `0` to `1` and vice versa.

Assignments

In assignments where the value being assigned is the result of an expression which comprises a string or number literal constant, the type of the result is defined as follows:

1. Strings are given the native string type, even for a single-character literal.[61]

2. Numbers are given the smallest possible primitive numeric type that will contain the literal without loss of information (or minimal loss of information for numbers with decimal or exponential parts). If this is smaller than the implementation-defined minimum precision used for the result of adding the literal to `0`, then the type of that minimum precision is used.

   If the constant is an integer, and no primitive integer binary type has sufficient precision to hold the number without loss of information, then the number is treated as a literal string (that is, as though it were enclosed in quotes). NetRexx arithmetic would then be used if it were involved in an arithmetic operation.

These rules can apply in assignment instructions, the initial assignment to the control variable in the **loop** instruction, or the assignment of a default value to the argument of a method; the result type may define the type of the variable (if new, or a method argument).

---

[61] *In the reference implementation, this is* `java.lang.String`.

Control variables in loops

In the **loop** instruction, if the control variable has a primitive integer type, and the increment (**by** value) has a primitive integer type, then binary arithmetic will be used for stepping the control variable, following the rules for binary arithmetic in expressions described above.

Similarly, if the control variable has a primitive integer type, and the end (**to**) value has a primitive integer type, then binary arithmetic will be used for the comparison that tests for loop termination.

Numeric instruction

The **numeric** instruction does not affect binary operations. It has the usual effects on operations carried out using NetRexx arithmetic.

Note: At all times (whether in binary classes or not) implementations may use primitive types and operations, and techniques such as late binding of types, as an optimization providing that the results obtained are identical to those defined in this language definition.

Binary constructors

NetRexx provides special constructors for implementation-defined primitive types that allow bit-wise construction of primitives. These *binary constructors* are especially useful for manipulating the binary encodings of individual characters.

The binary constructors follow the same syntax as other constructors, with the name being that of a primitive type. All binary constructors take one argument, which must have a primitive type.

The bits of the value of the argument are extended or truncated on the left to the same length as the bits required for the type of the constructor (following the usual binary rules of sign extension if the argument type is a signed numeric type), and a value with the type of the constructor is then constructed directly from those bits and returned.

Example:

This example illustrates types from the reference implementation, with 32-bit signed integers of type `int` and 16-bit Unicode characters of type `char`.

```
i=int 77     -- i is now the integer 77
c=char(i)    -- c is now the character 'M'
j=int(c)     -- j is now the integer 77
```

Note that the conversion

```
j=int c
```

would have failed, as “`M`” is not a number.

SECTION 38: EXCEPTIONS

Exceptional conditions, including errors, in NetRexx are handled by a mechanism called *Exceptions*. When an exceptional condition occurs, a *signal* takes place which may optionally be *caught* by an enclosing control construct, as detailed below.

An exception can be signalled by:

1. the program's environment, when some processing error occurs (such as running out of memory, or a problem discovered when reading or writing a file)
2. a method called by a NetRexx program (if, for example, it is passed incorrect arguments)
3. the **signal** instruction (see page 110).

In all cases, the signal is handled in exactly the same way. First, execution of the current clause ceases; no further operations within the clause will be carried out.[62] Next, an object that represents the exception is constructed. The type of the exception object is implementation-dependent, as described for the **signal** instruction (see page 110), and defines the type of the exception. The object constructed usually contains information about the Exception (such as a descriptive string).

Once the object has been constructed, all active **do** groups, **loop** loops, **if** constructs, and **select** constructs in the active method are "unwound", starting with the innermost, until the exception is caught by a control construct that specifies a suitable **catch** clause (see below) for handling the exception.

This unwinding takes place as follows:

1. No further clauses within the body of the construct will be executed (in this respect, the signal acts like a **leave** for the construct).
2. If a **catch** clause specifies a type to which the exception object can be assigned (that is, it matches or is a superclass of the type of exception object), then the *instructionlist* following that clause is executed, and the exception is considered to be handled (no further control constructs will be unwound). If more than one **catch** clause specifies a suitable type, the first is used.
3. The *instructionlist* following the **finally** clause for the construct, if any, is executed.
4. The **end** clause is executed, hence completing execution of the construct. (The only effect of this is that it is seen when tracing.)

---

62 This is the only case in which an expression will not be wholly evaluated, for example.

5. If the exception was handled, then execution resumes as though the construct completed normally. If it was not handled, then the process is repeated for any enclosing constructs.

If the exception is not caught by any of the control constructs enclosing the original point of the exception signal, then the current active method is terminated, without returning any data, and the exception is then signalled at the point where the method was invoked (that is, in the caller).

The process of unwinding control constructs and terminating the method is then repeated in each calling method until the exception is caught or the initial program invocation method (the main method) is terminated, in which case the program ends and the environment receives the signal (it would usually then display diagnostic information).

Syntax and example

The constructs that may be used to handle (catch) an exception are **do** groups, **loop** loops, and **select** constructs. Specifically, as shown in the syntax diagrams (*q.v.*), where the **end** clause can appear in these constructs, zero or more **catch** clauses can be used to define exception handlers, followed by zero or one **finally** clauses that describe "clean-up" code for the construct. The whole construct continues to be ended by an **end** clause.

The syntax of a **catch** clause is shown in the syntax diagrams. It always specifies an *exception* type, which may be qualified. It may optionally specify a symbol, *vare*, which is followed by an equals sign. This indicates that when the exception is caught then the object representing the exception will be assigned to the variable *vare*. If new, the type of the variable will be *exception*.

Here is an example of a program that handles some of the exceptions signalled by methods in the `Rexx` class; the **trace results** instruction is included to show the flow of execution:

```
trace results
do                    -- could be LOOP i=1 to 10, etc.
  say 1/arg
catch DivideException
  say 'Divide exception'
catch ex=NumberFormatException
  /* 'ex' is assigned the exception object */
  say 'Bad number for division:' ex.getMessage
finally
  say 'Done!'
end
```

In this example, if the argument passed to the program (and hence placed in `arg`) is a valid number, then its inverse is displayed. If the argument is 0, then "`Divide exception`" would be displayed. If the argument were an invalid number, the message describing the bad number would be displayed.

For any other exception (such as an `ExponentOverflowException`), the program would end and the environment would normally report the exception.

In **all** cases, the message "`Done!`" would be displayed; this would be true even if the body of the **do** construct executed a **return**, **leave**, or **iterate** instruction. Only an **exit** instruction (see page 79) would cause immediate termination of the construct (and the program).

Note: The **finally** keyword, like **otherwise** in the **select** construct, implies a semicolon after it, so the last **say** instruction in the example could have appeared on the same line as the **finally** without an intervening semicolon.

Exceptions after catch and finally clauses

If an exception is signalled in the *instructionlist* following a **catch** or **finally** clause, then the current exception is considered handled, the *instructionlist* is terminated, and the new exception is signalled. It will not be caught by **catch** clauses in the current construct. If it occurs in the *instructionlist* following a **catch** clause, then any **finally** instructions will be executed, as usual.

Similarly, executing a **return** or **exit** instruction within either of the *instructionlists* completes the handling of any pending signal.

Checked exceptions

NetRexx implementations may define certain exceptions as *checked exceptions*. These are exceptions that the implementation considers it useful to check; the checked exceptions that each method may signal are recorded. Within **do** groups, **loop** loops, and **select** constructs, for example, it is then possible to report if a **catch** clause tries to catch a checked exception that is not signalled within the body of the construct.

Checked exceptions that are signalled within a method (by a **signal** instruction or a method invocation) but not caught by a **catch** clause in the method are automatically added to the **signals** list for a method. Implementations that support checked exceptions are encouraged to provide options that list the uncaught checked exceptions for methods or enforce the explicit inclusion of some or all checked exceptions in the **signals** list on the method instruction.

In the reference implementation, all exceptions are checked except those that are subclasses of `java.lang.RuntimeException` *or* `java.lang.Error`. *These latter are considered so ubiquitous that almost all methods would signal them.*

Expressions assigned as the initial values of properties must not invoke methods that may signal checked exceptions.

The **strictsignal** *option on the* **options** *instruction may be used to enforce the inclusion of all uncaught checked exceptions in methods'* **signals** *lists; this may be used to assure that any uncaught checked exceptions are intentional.*

SECTION 39: METHODS FOR NETREXX STRINGS

This section describes the set of methods defined for the NetRexx string class, `Rexx`. These are called *built–in methods*, and include character manipulation, word manipulation, conversion, and arithmetic methods.

Implementations will also provide other methods for the `Rexx` class (for example, to implement the NetRexx operators or to provide constructors with primitive arguments), but these are not part of the NetRexx language.

General notes on the built-in methods:

1. All methods work on a NetRexx string of type `Rexx`; this is referred to by the name *string* in the descriptions of the methods. For example, if the `word` method were invoked using the term:

   ```
   "Three word phrase".word(2)
   ```

   then in the description of `word` the name *string* refers to the string “`Three word phrase`”, and the name *n* refers to the string “2”.
2. All method arguments are of type `Rexx` and all methods return a string of type `Rexx`; if a number is returned, it will be formatted as though 0 had been added with no rounding.
3. The first parenthesis in a method call must immediately follow the name of the method, with no space in between.
4. The parentheses in a method call can be omitted if no arguments are required and the method call is part of a *compound term* (see page 42).[63]
5. A position in a string is the number of a character in the string, where the first character is at position 1, *etc.*
6. Where arguments are optional, commas may only be included between arguments that are present (that is, trailing commas in argument lists are not permitted).
7. A *pad* argument, if specified, must be exactly one character long.
8. If a method has a sub-option selected by the first character of a string, that character may be in upper or lowercase.
9. Conversion between character encodings and decimal or hexadecimal is dependent on the machine representation (encoding) of characters and hence will return appropriately different results for Unicode, ASCII, EBCDIC, and other implementations.

---

[63] Unless an implementation-provided option to disallow parenthesis omission is in force.

The built-in methods

abbrev(info[,length])

returns 1 if *info* is equal to the leading characters of *string* and *info* is not less than the minimum length, *length*; 0 is returned if either of these conditions is not met. *length* must be a non-negative whole number; the default is the length of *info*.

Examples:

```
'Print'.abbrev('Pri')      == 1
'PRINT'.abbrev('Pri')      == 0
'PRINT'.abbrev('PRI',4)    == 0
'PRINT'.abbrev('PRY')      == 0
'PRINT'.abbrev('')         == 1
'PRINT'.abbrev('',1)       == 0
```

Note: A null string will always match if a length of 0 (or the default) is used. This allows a default keyword to be selected automatically if desired.

Example:

```
say 'Enter option:';   pull option .
select  /* keyword1 is to be the default */
  when 'keyword1'.abbrev(option) then ...
  when 'keyword2'.abbrev(option) then ...
     ...
  otherwise ...
  end
```

abs()

returns the absolute value of *string*, which must be a number.

Any sign is removed from the number, and it is then formatted by adding zero with a digits setting that is either nine or, if greater, the number of digits in the mantissa of the number (excluding leading insignificant zeros). Scientific notation is used, if necessary.

Examples:

```
'12.3'.abs                 == 12.3
' -0.307'.abs              == 0.307
'123.45E+16'.abs           == 1.2345E+18
'- 1234567.7654321'.abs == 1234567.7654321
```

b2x()

Binary to hexadecimal. Converts *string*, a string of at least one binary (`0` and/or `1`) digits, to an equivalent string of hexadecimal characters. The returned string will use uppercase Roman letters for the values A-F, and will not include any blanks.

If the number of binary digits in the string is not a multiple of four, then up to three `'0'` digits will be added on the left before conversion to make a total that is a multiple of four.

Examples:

```
'11000011'.b2x  == 'C3'
'10111'.b2x     == '17'
'0101'.b2x      == '5'
'101'.b2x       == '5'
'111110000'.b2x == '1F0'
```

center(length[,pad])

or

centre(length[,pad])

returns a string of length *length* with *string* centered in it, with *pad* characters added as necessary to make up the required length. *length* must be a non-negative whole number. The default *pad* character is blank. If the string is longer than *length*, it will be truncated at both ends to fit. If an odd number of characters are truncated or added, the right hand end loses or gains one more character than the left hand end.

Examples:

```
'ABC'.centre(7)               == '  ABC  '
'ABC'.center(8,'-')           == '--ABC---'
'The blue sky'.centre(8) == 'e blue s'
'The blue sky'.center(7) == 'e blue '
```

Note: This method may be called either `centre` or `center`, which avoids difficulties due to the difference between the British and American spellings.

changestr(needle, new)

returns a copy of *string* in which each occurrence of the *needle* string is replaced by the *new* string. Each unique (non-overlapping) occurrence of the *needle* string is changed, searching from left to right and starting from the first (leftmost) position in *string*. Only the original *string* is searched for the *needle*, and each character in *string* can only be included in one match of the *needle*.

If the *needle* is the null string, the result is a copy of *string*, unchanged.

Examples:

```
'elephant'.changestr('e','X')     == 'XlXphant'
'elephant'.changestr('ph','X')    == 'eleXant'
'elephant'.changestr('ph','hph')  == 'elehphant'
'elephant'.changestr('e','')      == 'lphant'
'elephant'.changestr('','!!')     == 'elephant'
```

The `countstr` method (see page 152) can be used to count the number of changes that could be made to a string in this fashion.

compare(target[,pad])

returns 0 if *string* and *target* are the same. If they are not, the returned number is positive and is the position of the first character that is not the same in both strings. If one string is shorter than the other, one or more *pad* characters are added on the right to make it the same length for the comparison. The default *pad* character is a blank.

Examples:

```
'abc'.compare('abc')        == 0
'abc'.compare('ak')         == 2
'ab '.compare('ab')         == 0
'ab '.compare('ab',' ')     == 0
'ab '.compare('ab','x')     == 3
'ab-- '.compare('ab','-')   == 5
```

copies(n)

returns *n* directly concatenated copies of *string*. *n* must be positive or 0; if 0, the null string is returned.

Examples:

```
'abc'.copies(3) == 'abcabcabc'
'abc'.copies(0) == ''
''.copies(2)    == ''
```

countstr(needle)

returns the count of non-overlapping occurrences of the *needle* string in *string*, searching from left to right and starting from the first (leftmost) position in *string*.

If the *needle* is the null string, `0` is returned.

Examples:

```
'elephant'.countstr('e')  == '2'
'elephant'.countstr('ph') == '1'
'elephant'.countstr('')   == '0'
```

The `changestr` method (see page 151) can be used to change occurrences of *needle* to some other string.

c2d()

Coded character to decimal. Converts the encoding of the character in *string* (which must be exactly one character) to its decimal representation. The returned string will be a non-negative number that represents the encoding of the character and will not include any sign, blanks, insignificant leading zeros, or decimal part.

Examples:

```
'M'.c2d  == '77'  -- ASCII or Unicode
'7'.c2d  == '247' -- EBCDIC
'\r'.c2d == '13'  -- ASCII or Unicode
'\0'.c2d == '0'
```

The `c2x` method (see page 152) can be used to convert the encoding of a character to a hexadecimal representation.

c2x()

Coded character to hexadecimal. Converts the encoding of the character in *string* (which must be exactly one character) to its hexadecimal representation (unpacks). The returned string will use uppercase Roman letters for the values A-F, and will not include any blanks. Insignificant leading zeros are removed.

Examples:

```
'M'.c2x  == '4D' -- ASCII or Unicode
'7'.c2x  == 'F7' -- EBCDIC
'\r'.c2x == 'D'  -- ASCII or Unicode
'\0'.c2x == '0'
```

The `c2d` method (see page 152) can be used to convert the encoding of a character to a decimal number.

datatype(option)

returns 1 if *string* matches the description requested with the *option*, or 0 otherwise. If *string* is the null string, 0 is always returned.

Only the first character of *option* is significant, and it may be in either uppercase or lowercase. The following *option* characters are recognized:

`A` (Alphanumeric); returns 1 if *string* only contains characters from the ranges “a-z”, “A-Z”, and “0-9”.

`B` (Binary); returns 1 if *string* only contains the characters “0” and/or “1”.

`D` (Digits); returns 1 if *string* only contains characters from the range “0-9”.

`L` (Lowercase); returns 1 if *string* only contains characters from the range “a-z”.

`M` (Mixed case); returns 1 if *string* only contains characters from the ranges “a-z” and “A-Z”.

`N` (Number); returns 1 if *string* is a syntactically valid NetRexx number that could be added to `'0'` without error,

`S` (Symbol); returns 1 if *string* only contains characters that are valid in non-numeric symbols (the alphanumeric characters and underscore), and does not start with a digit. Note that both uppercase and lowercase letters are permitted.

`U` (Uppercase); returns 1 if *string* only contains characters from the range “A-Z”.

`W` (Whole Number); returns 1 if *string* is a syntactically valid NetRexx number that can be added to `'0'` without error, and whose decimal part after that addition, with no rounding, is zero.

`X` (heXadecimal); returns 1 if *string* only contains characters from the ranges “a-f”, “A-F”, and “0-9”.

Examples:

```
'101'.datatype('B')      == 1
'12.3'.datatype('D')     == 0
'12.3'.datatype('N')     == 1
'12.3'.datatype('W')     == 0
'LaArca'.datatype('M')   == 1
''.datatype('M')         == 0
'Llanes'.datatype('L')   == 0
'3 d'.datatype('s')      == 1
'BCd3'.datatype('X')     == 1
'BCgd3'.datatype('X')    == 0
```

Note: The `datatype` method tests the meaning of the characters in a string, independent of the encoding of those characters. Extra letters and Extra digits cause `datatype` to return 0 except for the number tests ("`N`" and "`W`"), which treat extra digits whose value is in the range 0-9 as though they were the corresponding arabic numeral.

delstr(n[,length])

returns a copy of *string* with the sub-string of *string* that begins at the nth character, and is of length *length* characters, deleted. If *length* is not specified, or is greater than the number of characters from *n* to the end of the string, the rest of the string is deleted (including the nth character). *length* must be a non-negative whole number, and *n* must be a positive whole number. If *n* is greater than the length of *string*, the string is returned unchanged.

Examples:

```
'abcd'.delstr(3)     == 'ab'
'abcde'.delstr(3,2)  == 'abe'
'abcde'.delstr(6)    == 'abcde'
```

delword(n[,length])

returns a copy of *string* with the sub-string of *string* that starts at the nth word, and is of length *length* blank-delimited words, deleted. If *length* is not specified, or is greater than number of remaining words in the string, it defaults to be the remaining words in the string (including the nth word). *length* must be a non-negative whole number, and *n* must be a positive whole number. If *n* is greater than the number of words in *string*, the string is returned unchanged. The string deleted includes any blanks following the final word involved, but none of the blanks preceding the first word involved.

Examples:

```
'Now is the  time'.delword(2,2) == 'Now time'
'Now is the time '.delword(3)   == 'Now is '
'Now  time'.delword(5)          == 'Now  time'
```

d2c()

Decimal to coded character. Converts the *string* (a NetRexx *number*) to a single character, where the number is used as the encoding of the character.

string must be a non-negative whole number. An error results if the encoding described does not produce a valid character for the implementation (for example, if it has more significant bits than the implementation's encoding for characters).

Examples:

```
'77'.d2c   == 'M'  -- ASCII or Unicode
'+77'.d2c  == 'M'  -- ASCII or Unicode
'247'.d2c  == '7'  -- EBCDIC
'0'.d2c    == '\0'
```

d2x([n])

Decimal to hexadecimal. Returns a string of hexadecimal characters of length as needed or of length *n*, which is the hexadecimal (unpacked) representation of the decimal number. The returned string will use uppercase Roman letters for the values A-F, and will not include any blanks.

string must be a whole number, and must be non-negative unless *n* is specified, or an error will result. If *n* is not specified, the length of the result returned is such that there are no leading 0 characters, unless *string* was equal to 0 (in which case `'0'` is returned).

If *n* is specified it is the length of the final result in characters; that is, after conversion the input string will be sign-extended to the required length (negative numbers are converted assuming twos-complement form). If the number is too big to fit into *n* characters, it will be truncated on the left. *n* must be a non-negative whole number.

Examples:

```
'9'.d2x         == '9'
'129'.d2x       == '81'
'129'.d2x(1)    == '1'
'129'.d2x(2)    == '81'
'127'.d2x(3)    == '07F'
'129'.d2x(4)    == '0081'
'257'.d2x(2)    == '01'
'-127'.d2x(2)   == '81'
'-127'.d2x(4)   == 'FF81'
'12'.d2x(0)     == ''
```

exists(index)

returns 1 if *index* names a sub-value (see page 70) of *string* that has explicitly been assigned a value, or 0 otherwise.

Example:

Following the instructions:

```
vowel=0
vowel['a']=1
vowel['b']=1
vowel['b']=null -- drops previous assignment
```

then:

```
vowel.exists('a') == '1'
vowel.exists('b') == '0'
vowel.exists('c') == '0'
```

format([before[,after]])

formats (lays out) *string*, which must be a number.

The number, *string*, is first formatted by adding zero with a digits setting that is either nine or, if greater, the number of digits in the mantissa of the number (excluding leading insignificant zeros). If no arguments are given, the result is precisely that of this operation.

The arguments *before* and *after* may be specified to control the number of characters to be used for the integer part and decimal part of the result respectively. If either of these is omitted, or is `null`, the number of characters used will be as many as are needed for that part.

before must be a positive number; if it is larger than is needed to contain the integer part, that part is padded on the left with blanks to the requested length. If *before* is not large enough to contain the integer part of the number (including the sign, for negative numbers), an error results.

after must be a non-negative number; if it is not the same size as the decimal part of the number, the number will be rounded (or extended with zeros) to fit. Specifying 0 for *after* will cause the number to be rounded to an integer (that is, it will have no decimal part or decimal point).

Examples:

```
' - 12.73'.format              == '-12.73'
'0.000'.format                 == '0'
'3'.format(4)                  == '   3'
'1.73'.format(4,0)             == '   2'
'1.73'.format(4,3)             == '   1.730'
'-.76'.format(4,1)             == '  -0.8'
'3.03'.format(4)               == '   3.03'
' - 12.73'.format(null,4)      == '-12.7300'
```

Further arguments may be passed to the **format** method to control the use of exponential notation. The full syntax of the method is then:

format([before[,after[,explaces[,exdigits[,exform]]]]])

The first two arguments are as already described. The other three (*explaces*, *exdigits*, and *exform*) control the exponent part of the result. The default for any of the arguments may be selected by omitting them (if there are no arguments to be specified to their right) or by using the value `null`.

explaces must be a positive number; it sets the number of places (digits after the sign of the exponent) to be used for any exponent part, the default being to use as many as are needed. If *explaces* is specified and is not large enough to contain the exponent, an error results. If *explaces* is not zero and the exponent will be 0, then *explaces*+2 blanks are supplied for the exponent part of the result.

exdigits sets the trigger point for use of exponential notation. If, after the first formatting, the number of places needed before the decimal point exceeds *exdigits*, or if the absolute value of the result is less than `0.000001`, then exponential form will be used. The default is the number of digits in the mantissa of the number (excluding leading insignificant zeros); that is, exponential notation will not be used. The current setting of **numeric digits** may be used by specifying the special word `digits` (see page 118). If 0 is specified for *exdigits*, exponential notation is always used unless the exponent would be 0.

exform sets the form for exponential notation (if needed). *exform* may be either `'Scientific'` (the default) or `'Engineering'`. Only the first character of *exform* is significant and it may be in uppercase or in lowercase. The current setting of **numeric form** may be used by specifying the special word `form` (see page 118). If engineering form is in effect, up to three digits (plus sign) may be needed for the integer part of the result (*before*).

Examples:

```
'12345.73'.format(null,null,2,2) == '1.234573E+04'
'12345.73'.format(null,3,null,0) == '1.235E+4'
'1.234573'.format(null,3,null,0) == '1.235'
'123.45'.format(null,3,2,0)      == '1.235E+02'
'1234.5'.format(null,3,2,0,'e')  == '123.450E+01'
'1.2345'.format(null,3,2,0)      == '1.235     '
'12345.73'.format(null,null,3,6) == '12345.73'
'12345e+5'.format(null,3,0)      == '1234500000.000'
```

Implementation minimum: If exponents are supported in an implementation, then they must be supported for exponents whose absolute value is at least as large as the largest number that can be expressed as an exact integer in default precision, *i.e.*, 999999999. Therefore, values for *explaces* of up to 9 should also be supported.

insert(new[,n[,length[,pad]]])

inserts the string *new*, padded or truncated to length *length*, into a copy of the target *string* after the nth character; the string with any inserts is returned. *length* and *n* must be a non-negative whole numbers. If *n* is greater than the length of the target string, padding is added before the *new* string also. The default value for *n* is 0, which means insert before the beginning of the string. The default value for *length* is the length of *new*. The default *pad* character is a blank.

Examples:

```
'abc'.insert('123')           == '123abc'
'abcdef'.insert(' ',3)        == 'abc def'
'abc'.insert('123',5,6)       == 'abc  123   '
'abc'.insert('123',5,6,'+')   == 'abc++123+++'
'abc'.insert('123',0,5,'-')   == '123--abc'
```

lastpos(needle[,start])

returns the position of the last occurrence of the string *needle* in *string* (the "haystack"), searching from right to left. If the string *needle* is not found, or is the null string, 0 is returned. By default the search starts at the last character of *string* and scans backwards. This may be overridden by specifying *start*, the point at which to start the backwards scan. *start* must be a positive whole number, and defaults to the value *string*.length if larger than that value or if not specified.

Examples:

```
'abc def ghi'.lastpos(' ')   == 8
'abc def ghi'.lastpos(' ',7) == 4
'abcdefghi'.lastpos(' ')     == 0
'abcdefghi'.lastpos('cd')    == 3
```

left(length[,pad])

returns a string of length *length* containing the left-most *length* characters of *string*. The string is padded with *pad* characters (or truncated) on the right as needed. The default *pad* character is a blank. *length* must be a non-negative whole number. This method is exactly equivalent to *string*.substr(1, *length* [, *pad*]).

Examples:

```
'abc d'.left(8)      == 'abc d   '
'abc d'.left(8,'.')  == 'abc d...'
'abc defg'.left(6)   == 'abc de'
```

length()

returns the number of characters in *string*.

Examples:

```
'abcdefgh'.length == 8
''.length         == 0
```

lower([n[,length]])

returns a copy of *string* with any uppercase characters in the sub-string of *string* that begins at the nth character, and is of length *length* characters, replaced by their lowercase equivalent.

n must be a positive whole number, and defaults to 1 (the first character in *string*). If *n* is greater than the length of *string*, the string is returned unchanged.

length must be a non-negative whole number. If *length* is not specified, or is greater than the number of characters from *n* to the end of the string, the rest of the string (including the nth character) is assumed.

Examples:

```
'SumA'.lower         == 'suma'
'SumA'.lower(2)      == 'Suma'
'SuMB'.lower(1,1)    == 'suMB'
'SUMB'.lower(2,2)    == 'SumB'
''.lower             == ''
```

max(number)

returns the larger of *string* and *number*, which must both be numbers. If they compare equal (that is, when subtracted, the result is 0), then *string* is selected for the result.

The comparison is effected using a numerical comparison with a digits setting that is either nine or, if greater, the larger of the number of digits in the mantissas of the two numbers (excluding leading insignificant zeros).

The selected result is formatted by adding zero to the selected number with a digits setting that is either nine or, if greater, the number of digits in the mantissa of the number (excluding leading insignificant zeros). Scientific notation is used, if necessary.

Examples:

```
0.max(1)            ==1
'-1'.max(1)         ==1
'+1'.max(-1)        ==1
'1.0'.max(1.00)     =='1.0'
'1.00'.max(1.0)     =='1.00'
'123456700000'.max(1234567E+5)     == '123456700000'
'1234567E+5'.max('123456700000') == '1.234567E+11'
```

min(number)

returns the smaller of *string* and *number*, which must both be numbers. If they compare equal (that is, when subtracted, the result is 0), then *string* is selected for the result.

The comparison is effected using a numerical comparison with a digits setting that is either nine or, if greater, the larger of the number of digits in the mantissas of the two numbers (excluding leading insignificant zeros).

The selected result is formatted by adding zero to the selected number with a digits setting that is either nine or, if greater, the number of digits in the mantissa of the number (excluding leading insignificant zeros). Scientific notation is used, if necessary.

Examples:

```
0.min(1)              ==0
'-1'.min(1)           =='-1'
'+1'.min(-1)          =='-1'
'1.0'.min(1.00)       =='1.0'
'1.00'.min(1.0)       =='1.00'
'123456700000'.min(1234567E+5)     == '123456700000'
'1234567E+5'.min('123456700000') == '1.234567E+11'
```

overlay(new[,n[,length[,pad]]])

overlays the string *new*, padded or truncated to length *length*, onto a copy of the target *string* starting at the nth character; the string with any overlays is returned. Overlays may extend beyond the end of the original *string*. If *length* is specified it must be a non-negative whole number. If *n* is greater than the length of the target string, padding is added before the *new* string also. The default *pad* character is a blank, and the default value for *n* is 1. *n* must be greater than 0. The default value for *length* is the length of *new*.

Examples:

```
'abcdef'.overlay(' ',3)        == 'ab def'
'abcdef'.overlay('.',3,2)      == 'ab. ef'
'abcd'.overlay('qq')           == 'qqcd'
'abcd'.overlay('qq',4)         == 'abcqq'
'abc'.overlay('123',5,6,'+') == 'abc+123+++'
```

pos(needle[,start])

returns the position of the string *needle*, in *string* (the "haystack"), searching from left to right. If the string *needle* is not found, or is the null string, 0 is returned. By default the search starts at the first character of *string* (that is, *start* has the value 1). This may be overridden by specifying *start* (which must be a positive whole number), the point at which to start the search; if *start* is greater than the length of *string* then 0 is returned.

Examples:

```
'Saturday'.pos('day')      == 6
'abc def ghi'.pos('x')     == 0
'abc def ghi'.pos(' ')     == 4
'abc def ghi'.pos(' ',5)   == 8
```

reverse()

returns a copy of *string*, swapped end for end.

Examples:

```
'ABc.'.reverse          == '.cBA'
'XYZ '.reverse          == ' ZYX'
'Tranquility'.reverse   == 'ytiliuqnarT'
```

right(length[,pad])

returns a string of length *length* containing the right-most *length* characters of *string* – that is, padded with *pad* characters (or truncated) on the left as needed. The default *pad* character is a blank. *length* must be a non-negative whole number.

Examples:

```
'abc  d'.right(8)    == '   abc  d'
'abc def'.right(5)   == 'c def'
'12'.right(5,'0')    == '00012'
```

sequence(final)

returns a string of all characters, in ascending order of encoding, between and including the character in *string* and the character in *final*. *string* and *final* must be single characters; if *string* is greater than *final*, an error is reported.

Examples:

```
'a'.sequence('f')            == 'abcdef'
'\0'.sequence('\x03')        == '\x00\x01\x02\x03'
'\ufffe'.sequence('\uffff') == '\ufffe\uffff'
```

sign()

returns a number that indicates the sign of *string*, which must be a number. *string* is first formatted, just as though the operation "`string+0`" had been carried out with sufficient digits to avoid rounding. If the number then starts with `'-'` then `'-1'` is returned; if it is `'0'` then `'0'` is returned; and otherwise `'1'` is returned.

Examples:

```
'12.3'.sign     ==  1
'0.0'.sign      ==  0
' -0.307'.sign == -1
```

space([n[,pad]])

returns a copy of *string* with the blank-delimited words in *string* formatted with *n* (and only *n*) *pad* characters between each word. *n* must be a non-negative whole number. If *n* is 0, all blanks are removed. Leading and trailing blanks are always removed. The default for *n* is 1, and the default *pad* character is a blank.

Examples:

```
'abc  def  '.space         == 'abc def'
'  abc def '.space(3)      == 'abc   def'
'abc  def  '.space(1)      == 'abc def'
'abc  def  '.space(0)      == 'abcdef'
'abc  def  '.space(2,'+')  == 'abc++def'
```

strip([option[,char]])

returns a copy of *string* with Leading, Trailing, or Both leading and trailing characters removed, when the first character of *option* is L, T, or B respectively (these may be given in either uppercase or lowercase). The default is B. The second argument, *char*, specifies the character to be removed, with the default being a blank. If given, *char* must be exactly one character long.

Examples:

```
'  ab c  '.strip           == 'ab c'
'  ab c  '.strip('L')      == 'ab c  '
'  ab c  '.strip('t')      == '  ab c'
'12.70000'.strip('t',0) == '12.7'
'0012.700'.strip('b',0) == '12.7'
```

substr(n[,length[,pad]])

returns the sub-string of *string* that begins at the nth character, and is of length *length*, padded with *pad* characters if necessary. *n* must be a positive whole number, and *length* must be a non-negative whole number. If *n* is greater than *string*.`length`, then only pad characters can be returned.

If *length* is omitted it defaults to be the rest of the string. The default *pad* character is a blank.

Examples:

```
'abc'.substr(2)          == 'bc'
'abc'.substr(2,4)        == 'bc  '
'abc'.substr(5,4)        == '    '
'abc'.substr(2,6,'.') == 'bc....'
'abc'.substr(5,6,'.') == '......'
```

Note: In some situations the positional (numeric) patterns of parsing templates are more convenient for selecting sub-strings, especially if more than one sub-string is to be extracted from a string.

subword(n[,length])

returns the sub-string of *string* that starts at the nth word, and is up to *length* blank-delimited words long. *n* must be a positive whole number; if greater than the number of words in the string then the null string is returned. *length* must be a non-negative whole number. If *length* is omitted it defaults to be the remaining words in the string. The returned string will never have leading or trailing blanks, but will include all blanks between the selected words.

Examples:

```
'Now is the  time'.subword(2,2) == 'is the'
'Now is the  time'.subword(3)   == 'the  time'
'Now is the  time'.subword(5)   == ''
```

translate(tableo,tablei[,pad])

returns a copy of *string* with each character in *string* either unchanged or translated to another character.

The `translate` method acts by searching the input translate table, *tablei*, for each character in *string*. If the character is found in *tablei* (the first, leftmost, occurrence being used if there are duplicates) then the corresponding character in the same position in the output translate table, *tableo*, is used in the result string; otherwise the original character found in *string* is used. The result string is always the same length as *string*.

The translate tables may be of any length, including the null string. The output table, *tableo*, is padded with *pad* or truncated on the right as necessary to be the same length as *tablei*. The default *pad* is a blank.

Examples:

```
'abbc'.translate('&','b')             == 'a&&c'
'abcdef'.translate('12','ec')         == 'ab2d1f'
'abcdef'.translate('12','abcd','.')   == '12..ef'
'4123'.translate('abcd','1234')       == 'dabc'
'4123'.translate('hods','1234')       == 'shod'
```

Note: The last two examples show how the `translate` method may be used to move around the characters in a string. In these examples, any 4-character string could be specified as the first argument and its last character would be moved to the beginning of the string. Similarly, the term:

```
'gh.ef.abcd'.translate(19960827,'abcdefgh')
```

(which returns "`27.08.1996`") shows how a string (in this case perhaps a date) might be re-formatted and merged with other characters using the `translate` method.

trunc([n])

returns the integer part of *string*, which must be a number, with *n* decimal places (digits after the decimal point). *n* must be a non-negative whole number, and defaults to zero.

The number *string* is formatted by adding zero with a digits setting that is either nine or, if greater, the number of digits in the mantissa of the number (excluding leading insignificant zeros). It is then truncated to *n* decimal places (or trailing zeros are added if needed to make up the specified length). If *n* is 0 (the default) then an integer with no decimal point is returned. The result will never be in exponential form.

Examples:

```
'12.3'.trunc             == 12
'127.09782'.trunc(3)  == 127.097
'127.1'.trunc(3)       == 127.100
'127'.trunc(2)         == 127.00
'0'.trunc(2)           == 0.00
```

upper([n[,length]])

returns a copy of *string* with any lowercase characters in the sub-string of *string* that begins at the nth character, and is of length *length* characters, replaced by their uppercase equivalent.

n must be a positive whole number, and defaults to 1 (the first character in *string*). If *n* is greater than the length of *string*, the string is returned unchanged.

length must be a non-negative whole number. If *length* is not specified, or is greater than the number of characters from *n* to the end of the string, the rest of the string (including the nth character) is assumed.

Examples:

```
'Fou-Baa'.upper          == 'FOU-BAA'
'Mad Sheep'.upper        == 'MAD SHEEP'
'Mad sheep'.upper(5)     == 'Mad SHEEP'
'Mad sheep'.upper(5,1)  == 'Mad Sheep'
'Mad sheep'.upper(5,4)  == 'Mad SHEEp'
'tinganon'.upper(1,1)   == 'Tinganon'
''.upper                  == ''
```

verify(reference[,option[,start]])

verifies that *string* is composed only of characters from *reference*, by returning the position of the first character in *string* that is not also in *reference*. If all the characters were found in *reference*, 0 is returned.

The *option* may be either `'Nomatch'` (the default) or `'Match'`. Only the first character of *option* is significant and it may be in uppercase or in lowercase. If `'Match'` is specified, the position of the first character in *string* that **is** in *reference* is returned, or 0 is returned if none of the characters were found.

The default for *start* is 1 (that is, the search starts at the first character of *string*). This can be overridden by giving a different *start* point, which must be positive.

If *string* is the null string, the method returns 0, regardless of the value of the *option:*. Similarly if *start* is greater than *string*`.length`, 0 is returned.

If *reference* is the null string, then the returned value is the same as the value used for *start*, unless `'Match'` is specified as the *option*, in which case 0 is returned.

Examples:

```
'123'.verify('1234567890')          == 0
'1Z3'.verify('1234567890')          == 2
'AB4T'.verify('1234567890','M')     == 3
'1P3Q4'.verify('1234567890','N',3)  == 4
'ABCDE'.verify('','n',3)            == 3
'AB3CD5'.verify('1234567890','m',4) == 6
```

word(n)

returns the nth blank-delimited word in *string*. *n* must be positive. If there are fewer than *n* words in *string*, the null string is returned. This method is exactly equivalent to *string*`.subword(`*n*`,1)`.

Examples:

```
'Now is the time'.word(3) == 'the'
'Now is the time'.word(5) == ''
```

wordindex(n)

returns the character position of the nth blank-delimited word in *string*. *n* must be positive. If there are fewer than *n* words in the string, 0 is returned.

Examples:

```
'Now is the time'.wordindex(3) == 8
'Now is the time'.wordindex(6) == 0
```

wordlength(string,n)

returns the length of the nth blank-delimited word in *string*. *n* must be positive. If there are fewer than *n* words in the string, 0 is returned.

Examples:

```
'Now is the time'.wordlength(2)    == 2
'Now comes the time'.wordlength(2) == 5
'Now is the time'.wordlength(6)    == 0
```

wordpos(phrase[,start])

searches *string* for the first occurrence of the sequence of blank-delimited words *phrase*, and returns the word number of the first word of *phrase* in *string*. Multiple blanks between words in either *phrase* or *string* are treated as a single blank for the comparison, but otherwise the words must match exactly. Similarly, leading or trailing blanks on either string are ignored. If *phrase* is not found, or contains no words, 0 is returned.

By default the search starts at the first word in *string*. This may be overridden by specifying *start* (which must be positive), the word at which to start the search.

Examples:

```
'now is the time'.wordpos('the')        == 3
'now is the time'.wordpos('The')        == 0
'now is the time'.wordpos('is the')     == 2
'now is the time'.wordpos('is    the') == 2
'now is the time'.wordpos('is  time')   == 0
'To be or not to be'.wordpos('be')      == 2
'To be or not to be'.wordpos('be',3)    == 6
```

words()

returns the number of blank-delimited words in *string*.

Examples:

```
'Now is the time'.words == 4
' '.words               == 0
''.words                == 0
```

x2b()

Hexadecimal to binary. Converts *string* (a string of at least one hexadecimal characters) to an equivalent string of binary digits. Hexadecimal characters may be any decimal digit character (0-9) or any of the first six alphabetic characters (a-f), in either lowercase or uppercase.

string may be of any length; each hexadecimal character with be converted to a string of four binary digits. The returned string will have a length that is a multiple of four, and will not include any blanks.

Examples:

```
'C3'.x2b  == '11000011'
'7'.x2b   == '0111'
'1C1'.x2b == '000111000001'
```

x2c()

Hexadecimal to coded character. Converts the *string* (a string of hexadecimal characters) to a single character (packs). Hexadecimal characters may be any decimal digit character (0-9) or any of the first six alphabetic characters (a-f), in either lowercase or uppercase.

string must contain at least one hexadecimal character; insignificant leading zeros are removed, and the string is then padded with leading zeros if necessary to make a sufficient number of hexadecimal digits to describe a character encoding for the implementation.

An error results if the encoding described does not produce a valid character for the implementation (for example, if it has more significant bits than the implementation's encoding for characters).

Examples:

```
'004D'.x2c == 'M' -- ASCII or Unicode
'4d'.x2c   == 'M' -- ASCII or Unicode
'A2'.x2c   == 's' -- EBCDIC
'0'.x2c    == '\0'
```

The `d2c` method (see page 155) can be used to convert a NetRexx number to the encoding of a character.

x2d([n])

Hexadecimal to decimal. Converts the *string* (a string of hexadecimal characters) to a decimal number, without rounding. If *string* is the null string, 0 is returned.

If *n* is not specified, *string* is taken to be an unsigned number.

Examples:

```
'0E'.x2d     == 14
'81'.x2d     == 129
'F81'.x2d    == 3969
'FF81'.x2d   == 65409
'c6f0'X.x2d == 240
```

If *n* is specified, *string* is taken as a signed number expressed in *n* hexadecimal characters. If the most significant (left-most) bit is zero then the number is positive; otherwise it is a negative number in twos-complement form. In both cases it is converted to a NetRexx number which may, therefore, be negative. If *n* is 0, 0 is always returned.

If necessary, *string* is padded on the left with `'0'` characters (note, not "sign-extended"), or truncated on the left, to length *n* characters; (that is, as though *string*`.right(`*n*`, '0')` had been executed.)

Examples:

```
'81'.x2d(2)     == -127
'81'.x2d(4)     == 129
'F081'.x2d(4) == -3967
'F081'.x2d(3) == 129
'F081'.x2d(2) == -127
'F081'.x2d(1) == 1
'0031'.x2d(0) == 0
```

The `c2d` method (see page 152) can be used to convert a character to a decimal representation of its encoding.

Appendix A: NetRexx Syntax Diagrams

This appendix collects together the syntax diagrams of the NetRexx instructions presented earlier in this book. They include general terms defined on the following pages:

term	Page 41.
expression	Page 56.
instruction	Page 73.
pattern	Page 122.
string	Page 33.
symbol	Page 35.
template	Page 122.

Other terms specific to individual instructions are explained in the section describing that instruction.

Method call:

symbol **(** [*expression* [, *expression*] ...] **)** ;

Assignment:

assignment ;

where *assignment* is:

term = *expression*

Keyword instructions:

class *name* [*visibility*] [*modifier*] [**binary**]
[**extends** *classname*]
[**uses** *useslist*]
[**implements** *interfacelist*] ;

where *visibility* is one of:

private
public

and *modifier* is one of:

abstract
final
interface

and *useslist* and *interfacelist* are lists of one or more *classnames*, separated by commas.

do [**label** *name*] [**protect** *term*] ;
instructionlist
[**catch** [*vare* =] *exception* ; *instructionlist*] ...
[**finally** [;] *instructionlist*]
end [*name*] ;

where *name* is a non-numeric *symbol*

and *instructionlist* is zero or more *instructions*.

---

exit [*expression*] ;

---

if *expression* [;]
then [;] *instruction*
[**else** [;] *instruction*]

---

import *name* ;

where *name* is one or more non-numeric *symbols* separated by periods, with an optional trailing period.

---

iterate [*name*] ;

where *name* is a non-numeric *symbol*.

---

leave [*name*] ;

where *name* is a non-numeric *symbol*.

loop [**label** *name*] [**protect** *termp*] [*repetitor*] [*conditional*] ;
instructionlist
[**catch** [*vare* =] *exception* ; *instructionlist*] ...
[**finally** [;] *instructionlist*]
end [*name*] ;

where *repetitor* is one of:

varc = *expri* [**to** *exprt*] [**by** *exprb*] [**for** *exprf*]
varo **over** *termo*
for *exprr*
forever

and *conditional* is either of:

while *exprw*
until *expru*

and *name* is a non-numeric *symbol*

and *instructionlist* is zero or more *instructions*

and *expri*, *exprt*, *exprb*, *exprf*, *exprr*, *exprw*, and *expru* are *expressions*.

method *name*[([*arglist*])]
[*visibility*] [*modifier*] [**protect**]
[**returns** *termr*]
[**signals** *signallist*] ;

where *arglist* is a list of one or more *assignments*, separated by commas

and *visibility* is one of:

inheritable
private
public

and *modifier* is one of:

abstract
constant
final
native
static

and *signallist* is a list of one or more *terms*, separated by commas.

nop ;

---

numeric { **digits** [*exprd*] | **form** [**scientific** | **engineering**] } ;

where *exprd* is an *expression*.

---

options *wordlist* ;

where *wordlist* is one or more *symbols* separated by blanks.

---

package *name* ;

where *name* is one or more non-numeric *symbols* separated by periods.

---

parse *term* *template* ;

where *template* is one or more non-numeric *symbols* separated by blanks or *patterns*

and a *pattern* is one of:

literalstring

[*indicator*] *number*

[*indicator*] **(** *symbol* **)**

and *indicator* is one of **+**, **–**, or **=**.

properties [*visibility*] [*modifier*] ;

where *visibility* is one of:

inheritable
private
public

and *modifier* is one of:

constant
static
volatile

and there must be at least one *visibility* or *modifier* keyword.

---

return [*expression*] ;

---

say [*expression*] ;

---

select [**label** *name*] [**protect** *termp*] ;
whenlist
[**otherwise** [;] *instructionlist*]
[**catch** [*vare* =] *exception* ; *instructionlist*] ...
[**finally** [;] *instructionlist*]
end [*name*] ;

where *name* is a non-numeric *symbol*

and *whenlist* is one or more *whenconstruct*s

and *whenconstruct* is:

when *expression* [;] **then** [;] *instruction*

and *instructionlist* is zero or more *instruction*s.

---

signal *term* ;

trace [**all** | **methods** | **off** | **results**] **;**

Appendix B: A Sample NetRexx Program

This appendix includes a short program, called `qtime`, which is an example of a "real" NetRexx program. The programs included elsewhere in this book have been contrived to illustrate specific points. By contrast, `qtime` is a simple but useful tool that genuinely improves the human factors of computer systems. People frequently wish to know the time of day, and this program presents this information in a natural way.

The style used for this example is the same as that used throughout the book, with all symbols except those describing classes being written in lower case. Other NetRexx programming styles are possible, of course; NetRexx syntax is designed to permit a wide variety of styles with a minimum of punctuation.

The `qtime` program is a modification of one of the first Rexx programs ever written (much of the program is identical). The main changes are:

- Indexed variables (brackets notation) are used instead of Rexx stems.
- The `word` method from the `Rexx` class is used instead of the `word` Rexx built-in function.
- The Java `Date` class is used to determine the current time.

qtime.nrx – Query Time

```
/*----------------------------------------------------------*/
/* qtime.nrx.  This program displays the time in English.  */
/* If "?" is given as the first argument word then the     */
/* program displays a description of itself.               */
/*----------------------------------------------------------*/

/*--------- First process any argument words -------------*/
parse arg parm .             /* get the first argument word */
select
  when parm='?' then tell                  /* say what we do */
  when parm=''  then nop        /* OK (no first argument) */
  otherwise
    say 'The only valid argument to QTIME is "?".  The word'
    say 'that you supplied ("'parm'") has been ignored.'
    tell        /* usually helpful to describe the program */
  end

/*-------- Now start processing in earnest ---------------*/
/* Nearness phrases - using associative array lookup      */
near=''                                        /* default */
near[0]=''                                       /* exact */
near[1]=' just gone';  near[2]=' just after'     /* after */
near[3]=' nearly';     near[4]=' almost'        /* before */

/* Extract the hours, minutes, and seconds from the time. */
/* Use the Java Date class to get the time-of-day.        */
parse Date() . . . now .      /* time is the fourth word */
parse now hour':'min':'sec

if sec>29 then min=min+1                /* round up minutes */
mod=min//5             /* where we are in 5-minute bracket */
out="It's"near[mod]          /* start building the result */
if min>32 then hour=hour+1         /* we are TO the hour... */
min=min+2   /* shift minutes to straddle a 5-minute point */

/* Now special-case the result for Noon and Midnight.     */
if hour//12=0 & min//60<=4 then do
  if hour=12 then say out 'Noon.'
             else say out 'Midnight.'
  exit                           /* we are finished here */
  end
```

continued...

```
/* Find five-minute segment and convert to 12-hour clock. */
min=min-(min//5)                        /* find nearest 5 mins */
if hour>12
 then hour=hour-12                 /* get rid of 24-hour clock */
 else if hour=0 then hour=12 /* .. and allow for midnight */

/* Determine the phrase to use for each 5-minute segment. */
select
  when min= 0 then nop                  /* add "o'clock" later */
  when min=60 then min=0                                /* ditto */
  when min= 5 then out=out 'five past'
  when min=10 then out=out 'ten past'
  when min=15 then out=out 'a quarter past'
  when min=20 then out=out 'twenty past'
  when min=25 then out=out 'twenty-five past'
  when min=30 then out=out 'half past'
  when min=35 then out=out 'twenty-five to'
  when min=40 then out=out 'twenty to'
  when min=45 then out=out 'a quarter to'
  when min=50 then out=out 'ten to'
  when min=55 then out=out 'five to'
  end

numbers='one two three four five six'-  /* (continuation) */
  'seven eight nine ten eleven twelve '
out=out numbers.word(hour)              /* add the hour number */
if min=0 then out=out "o'clock"   /* and o'clock if exact */

say out'.'                         /* display the final result */
exit

/*--------------------------------------------------------*/
/* Tell: function that describes the use of the program.  */
/*--------------------------------------------------------*/
method tell static
 say 'QTIME displays the current time in natural English.'
 say 'Call without any arguments to display the time, or'
 say 'with "?" to display this information.'
 say 'British English idioms are used in this program.'
 say /* space -- we are about to continue and show time.  */
 return

/* Mike Cowlishaw,  December 1979 - January 1985          */
/* NetRexx version March 1996                             */
```

Index

Special Characters

C

D

E

F

G

H

I

J

K

L

O

P

Q

R

T

U

V